cPanel: User Guide and Tutorial

Get the most from cPanel with this easy-to-follow guide

D1556669

Aric Pedersen

BIRMINGHAM - MUMBAI

cPanel: User Guide and Tutorial

Get the most from cPanel with this easy-to-follow guide

First published: March 2006

Production Reference: 1030306

Published by Packt Publishing Ltd.
32 Lincoln Road
Olton
Birmingham, B27 6PA, UK.

ISBN 1-904811-92-2

www.packtpub.com

Cover Design by www.visionwt.com

Credits

Author
Aric Pedersen

Reviewer
Tad Boomer

Technical Editor
Rushabh Sanghavi

Editorial Manager
Dipali Chittar

Development Editor
David Barnes

Indexer
Ashutosh Pande

Proofreader
Chris Smith

Production Coordinator
Manjiri Nadkarni

Cover Designer
Helen Wood

About the Author

Aric Pedersen has been using cPanel on a daily basis for over six years both as an end user for his own websites and as a systems administrator. He currently works as a systems administrator for several hosting companies and also for Netenberg.com, the creators of Fantastico Deluxe (a popular script auto-installer for cPanel). Aric has been providing companies and end users with web hosting and related documentation for several years.

Though my name is on the front of this book, this project was not completed alone and I would like to take the time to thank a few people.

To my mother and Allen: My sincerest thanks for your support, now and always. I love both of you.

To Tony: Thanks for making me realize how much this thing really needed to get turned into a book!

To Manny: Thanks for taking that first chance and hiring me.

To John/Jack, Esq. III: People like you fight to keep America free so people like me can write stuff like this even if people like you don't understand a word of it! ☺ I owe you.

To my publisher: This book wouldn't be half as good as it is without your invaluable assistance.

I would also like to thank the hundreds of people who helped me when I was first learning how cPanel worked. This book is my attempt to give back to the community.

Finally, thanks to YOU for purchasing this book!

Table of Contents

Preface

This book is designed to provide in-depth information for anyone who needs assistance with cPanel web hosting software. If you've never managed your own website before you will be able to confidently use the many features cPanel provides after reading this book. Even intermediate and advanced users of cPanel will likely learn many tips and tricks that will enable them to work both faster and smarter.

What This Book Covers

Chapter 1: Introduction to cPanel Hosting

Before diving into the many features, you will learn:

- What cPanel is and what it is used for

- What tools you will need to get started working with cPanel and your website

- How to locate a web host that offers cPanel and what to look for in a good host

Chapter 2: Getting Started with cPanel

Start learning a few things about cPanel:

- Access cPanel in several different ways

- Familiarize yourself with the main cPanel interface

- Learn about some of the features of your cPanel account

Chapter 3: FTP and cPanel's File Manager

In this chapter you will discover most of the methods that cPanel provides to enable you to transfer files to and from your web hosting account:

- Discuss methods of uploading files to your hosting account

- Learn about the types of FTP clients available

- Learn how to work with FTP

- Accessing the main FTP account

- Creating FTP accounts and placing limits on those accounts

- Deleting FTP accounts

- Checking FTP quotas for accounts you create

- Managing Anonymous FTP access

- Monitoring FTP access and killing FTP sessions

- SFTP (Secure FTP)

- FXP (File Exchange Protocol)

- Navigating your site with the cPanel file manager

- Uploading files and downloading files, editing and managing files with the file manager

- WYSIWYG HTML editing via WYSIWYG Pro in the file manager

Chapter 4: Working with Mail

Dive into the many features cPanel offers for working with e-mail:

- Why you may want to manage your own e-mail accounts

- How to setup and manage POP3 and IMAP e-mail accounts

- How to create e-mail forwarders and forward all e-mail from one account to another

- Ways to combat spam and viruses using features available in cPanel

- How to work with web mail

- How to manage mailing lists

- The more advanced features cPanel provides for working with e-mail (changing MX records, tracing mail, etc.)

Chapter 5: Working with Databases

In this chapter we will explore the wonderful world of databases:

- What databases are and what they are used for

- How to work with both MySQL and PostgreSQL databases in cPanel to handle administrative tasks

- Creating databases

- Creating database users

- Adding users to databases

- Common connection settings for databases

- Deleting databases and users

- Checking for damage, repairing, and optimizing databases

- Basics of working with databases using phpMyAdmin or phpPgAdmin

- Backing up databases with phpMyAdmin or phpPgAdmin

Chapter 6: Controlling Access to and Organizing Your Data

In this chapter, you will learn how to manage access to and organize your site using numerous cPanel tools:

- Change your main cPanel password
- Create and manage subdomains
- What redirects are and why you might use them
- Enable hotlink protection and learn how to use it
- Manage leech protection
- Password-protect directories
- Stop problem users from visiting your site with the IP deny manager
- Create custom error messages

Chapter 7: Keeping an Eye on Account Activity

cPanel offers a number of features designed to allow you to keep track of what is happening in your account. In this chapter we will focus on:

- How to work with the various web statistics packages that cPanel offers
- How to disable and re-enable web statistics packages using the Stats Manager
- When and how to use your site's raw web logs
- How to keep track of the disk space your files are taking up
- How to use your cPanel error log to track down problems

Chapter 8: Backing up and Restoring Data

cPanel includes a number of tools that can help you get your site up and running again quickly in the event of data loss:

- What backups are and why they are so important
- How to use cPanel to back up the data in your account
- Automated backup methods
- How to use cPanel to restore the data that you've backed up
- What to do if you do not have a backup and need to restore the data in your account

Chapter 9: Working with Scripts

Regardless of your level of expertise, there will probably come a time when you want to add content or features to your website without spending days or weeks coding something or paying someone to create the content for you. This is where pre-coded web scripts may come in handy. In this chapter we will cover:

- What scripts are and what you might want to use them for

- What scripts cPanel offers for installation and how to install them

- Some important advice concerning working with scripts.

Chapter 10: Advanced cPanel Features

You've mastered the basics and are still hungry for more, so in this chapter, we will explore:

- How to enable and disable FrontPage Extensions and learn why you may or may not need them

- Creating and managing Add-on and Parked Domains

- Creating Cron jobs and learning what they can be used for

- The basics of working with SSH/Telnet

- Editing MIME Types and learning what they are used for

- Adding Apache Handlers and learning their uses

- The cPanel interface for creating and storing OpenPGP Keys

- How to manage SSL certificates using cPanel

- The advanced network tools cPanel offers

- What cPanel Pro is and what new features it can provide

Chapter 11: Site and Account Security

You know how to use the features in your cPanel account and now it is time to learn how to protect yourself and your account data. Specifically, we will cover the following:

- What hacking is and why you may be at risk

- What you can do to protect yourself and your site from attack

- What to do if your site is hacked

Chapter 12: Third-Party Additions to cPanel

This chapter will cover most common cPanel additions, and you will discover:

- Many popular cPanel themes and learn about what makes them unique

- A number of popular third-party add-ons for cPanel and learn how they work

Chapter 13: Useful Tools and Links and the Final Curtain Call

You've learned how to use the tools cPanel gives you. In this chapter you will find several great links for tools you can use for:

- FTP clients

- More cPanel information

- Basic webmaster and scripting assistance

- Domain, DNS, and Site Monitoring tools

- Password-storing programs

The Changing Nature of cPanel

While the information in this book is as current as possible at the time of its publication (covering cPanel 10.8.1), the features and functions of cPanel may be different from what is described in this book. The primary reasons for this are:

- cPanel is constantly being updated and revised to add new features and fix bugs. New features may be added or existing features extended or rearranged.

- Not all web hosts offer all features mentioned in this guide with all hosting plans. This is particularly true of some of the third-party add-ons that will be discussed. If you have questions about what features your web host offers, please contact them directly.

- Some web hosts may use a different default theme for cPanel than the one you see in this book (XSkin). Please see Chapter 12 for some screenshots of other themes that your host might offer.

Additional Assistance

If you find that you need additional information or assistance with cPanel there are several places you can turn to for help.

The first place to go if you have any questions is your web hosting company. They should be able to answer almost any question you have concerning cPanel or any web hosting plan features. Please be sure to follow your web host's support procedures when asking for assistance.

cPanel Inc., the makers of cPanel also maintain a customer-to-customer general support forum `http://forums.cpanel.net/`. This forum is *not* designed as a main means of support for cPanel, but is a good place to go if you have questions or concerns that your web host cannot answer. Often you can find answers to commonly asked questions by searching the forum, so make sure you try that before attempting to post a question.

cPanel Inc. also maintains some very basic (and typically very outdated) documentation. The online version of this documentation can be found at `http://www.cpanel.net/docs/cpanel/`. You may also be able to find this documentation as a link directly from the main screen of the cPanel interface (depending on the theme your web host provides). A PDF version of this documentation can be downloaded from `http://www.cpdocs.com/docs/pdf/cpanel`. Note that PDF files require a PDF reader such as the free Adobe Reader program, which you can obtain from `http://www.adobe.com/products/acrobat/readstep2.html`.

Conventions

In this book, you will find a number of styles of text that distinguish between different kinds of information. Here are some examples of these styles, and an explanation of their meaning.

There are three styles for code. Code words in text are shown as follows: "We can include other contexts through the use of the `include` directive."

A block of code will be set as follows:

```
<? header ("Location: http://domain.com/scriptdir/"); ?>
<html>
<title>Page Title</title>
<head></head>
<body></body>
</html>
```

When we wish to draw your attention to a particular part of a code block, the relevant lines or items will be made bold:

```
<? header ("Location: http://domain.com/scriptdir/"); ?>
<html>
<title>Page Title</title>
<head></head>
<body></body>
</html>
```

New terms and **important words** are introduced in a bold-type font. Words that you see on the screen, in menus or dialog boxes for example, appear in our text like this: "clicking the Next button moves you to the next screen".

> Warnings or important notes appear in a box like this.

Tips and tricks appear like this.

Reader Feedback

Feedback from our readers is always welcome. Let us know what you think about this book, what you liked or may have disliked. Reader feedback is important for us to develop titles that you really get the most out of.

To send us general feedback, simply drop an e-mail to `feedback@packtpub.com`, making sure to mention the book title in the subject of your message.

If there is a book that you need and would like to see us publish, please send us a note in the SUGGEST A TITLE form on www.packtpub.com or e-mail suggest@packtpub.com.

If there is a topic that you have expertise in and you are interested in either writing or contributing to a book, see our author guide on www.packtpub.com/authors.

Customer Support

Now that you are the proud owner of a Packt book, we have a number of things to help you to get the most from your purchase.

Errata

Although we have taken every care to ensure the accuracy of our contents, mistakes do happen. If you find a mistake in one of our books—maybe a mistake in text or code—we would be grateful if you would report this to us. By doing this you can save other readers from frustration, and help to improve subsequent versions of this book. If you find any errata, report them by visiting http://www.packtpub.com/support, selecting your book, clicking on the Submit Errata link, and entering the details of your errata. Once your errata have been verified, your submission will be accepted and the errata added to the list of existing errata. The existing errata can be viewed by selecting your title from http://www.packtpub.com/support.

Questions

You can contact us at questions@packtpub.com if you are having a problem with some aspect of the book, and we will do our best to address it.

1

Introduction to cPanel Hosting

The cPanel web hosting software is an easy-to-use, feature-rich tool for managing your website. But before we dive into all of cPanel's features, we need to have a basic idea about cPanel—What is it used for, what tools will you need to get started working with cPanel, how to locate a web host that offers cPanel, and what to look for in a good host.

So let's start by learning a little bit about what exactly is cPanel.

Webmaster, Meet cPanel…

Once you've decided that you want to create your own website, you have a lot of work ahead. You need to design content and figure out how to upload it to your site. Then you need to attract people to your site and manage any other features that your web host may offer such as e-mail, databases, subdomains, site security, etc. If you have no previous experience with handling any of this, it can be quite overwhelming.

cPanel is a web hosting control software that can be accessed using any modern web browser. It is designed to make the complex task of managing your hosting account easy. With the aid of cPanel and this book you should be able to get your new site up and running in no time.

What Tools Will You Need?

These are a few things which you will need before you start working with cPanel:

- **Private Internet Access**: You need to be able to freely access the Internet from a private location. For security reasons you should never try to access your cPanel account or work on your website from a public location like a library, school, or job.

- **A modern web browser**: cPanel works well in any recent web browser like Internet Explorer 5.5+, Netscape 7+, Mozilla, Firefox, Safari, or Opera. If you are using an older web browser you should upgrade if you want to use cPanel.

In addition, you may also want to make sure you have access to some of the following optional tools:

- **An HTML editor**: Such programs make it easier to create or edit files that are part of your website.

- **An FTP client**: This sort of program is used to upload, download, and manage files on your website. A client that supports **SFTP (Secure FTP)** is a bonus.

- **More than one modern web browser**: This can be handy to test your new website to make sure it looks the same on a wide variety of browsers.

- **An e-mail program**: If your hosting account includes e-mail, you will most likely find managing e-mail easier if you use a dedicated e-mail program rather than web-based e-mail programs.

You can find a list of commonly used tools and resources in Chapter 12.

Finding cPanel Web Hosting

If you don't already have a web host that offers cPanel, then the first order of business will be to locate one. There are probably tens of thousands of web hosts that offer cPanel to their clients. How do you go about finding the one that is right for you?

Types of Web Hosting

There are several different kinds of web hosting options, and it is important to understand the difference between them before you begin looking for a host.

The most common type of web hosting (and generally the cheapest) is **Shared Hosting**. Shared Hosting means that there are many websites hosted on a single web server. A web server is a special computer that handles storing and displaying websites. For most people who are looking to host a website for the first time or those who are concerned about the cost, shared hosting is the best choice. Since many websites are served from a single machine, the costs are generally lower than other hosting options. Costs vary from 0 to 40 USD per month on average.

However, shared hosting does have some drawbacks. The more sites a web server hosts, the more likely it is that your website may react sluggishly, since there are many demands on the web server. If you decide to purchase a shared web hosting account, you should ask your host what kind of hardware they host accounts on. Faster machines with more RAM are preferable. For example, a Dual Xeon CPU server with 2 GB of RAM will generally perform better than an old single Celeron CPU server with 512 MB of RAM. Just as important as knowing the server hardware, is getting a sense of how many shared hosting accounts your host will put on a server before considering it full—the fewer, the better.

The next type of web hosting is often referred to as **Reseller Hosting**. This is similar to shared hosting, except that you are allowed to resell shared hosting accounts to others. Reseller hosting allows you to start your own web hosting business. The average cost of a reseller hosting plan tends to fall between 20 and 60 USD a month. For those people who want to start a web hosting business but who do not have money for a VPS or dedicated server, reseller hosting is a good choice. The drawback is that like shared hosting, there may be many reseller hosting accounts on a server, each with many resold accounts. Knowing more about what kind of web server you will be hosted on is important.

On servers that contain resellers, the actual number of shared hosting accounts may vary widely, depending on how many accounts each reseller has. Many hosts do not require that you actually resell accounts if you buy a reseller plan. If so, then it is a good *step-up* from standard shared hosting since you can typically host many domains under a single reseller account with no extra fees involved. In addition, you get more control over the domains you manage in a reseller plan.

Some hosts will also offer **VPS/VDS hosting** and perhaps even **Dedicated Servers**. VPS (Virtual Private Server) and VDS (Virtual Dedicated Server) hosting are different names for the same type of hosting accounts. Such accounts use special software to take a single physical web server and divide it into two or more separate virtual web servers. Each virtual server acts as if it is a completely separate machine. Each virtual machine gets a guaranteed amount of the physical server resources including use of the CPU and disk space. VPS/VDS accounts have many of the advantages of dedicated servers without the higher cost. A VPS/VDS account may cost from 30 to 120 USD a month on average.

If you purchase a dedicated server, you receive an entire web server with no other accounts on it. Most of the time dedicated servers also permit you system administrator access (which allows you complete control over the server). Dedicated servers on average cost between 100 and 500 USD a month.

Windows versus Linux Hosting

In addition to the variation in types of hosting you can buy, some web hosts may offer both Linux and Windows operating system hosting. Some people who are new to web hosting may think that if they run Windows at home on their computer that they need Windows hosting. This is not true. Linux hosting plans typically cost less than Windows hosting plans due to the relative costs of the operating systems (Linux is often free and Windows costs money). cPanel only runs on Linux at this time, though Windows and Mac OS X versions are being prepared.

Hunting for Hosting

Now that you understand the difference between the various sorts of hosting you can purchase, you're ready to start looking for a host for your website. There are many different places you can look for information about hosting companies and hosting plans. Of course, you can visit Google (http://google.com/) and search for cPanel hosting to find some web hosts, but just because a host appears near the top of the search results does not mean that it will be the best host for your needs.

Finding the right host requires a good deal of research and perhaps even a bit of luck. There are so many web hosts that it is impossible to compare them all. A good general starting place is Web Hosting Talk (often referred to as *WHT*), `http://webhostingtalk.com/`. This forum is one of the busiest web hosting-related sites on the Internet and it attracts many web hosts and customers. For example, if you are looking for shared hosting, a good place to start is the shared hosting advertising area, `http://webhostingtalk.com/forumdisplay.php?f=4`. You can also sign up for a free account and talk to others about web hosting and web hosts.

If you are looking for an answer to a particular question you should always try to use the search feature first before posting, since your question may have already been answered. If you find a web host with a plan that looks interesting, do a search and see what others think of that host. If you find a web host with a very cheap plan but you find that there are a lot of negative comments about it, then you might want to consider finding another host.

Another place to go if you are looking for cPanel web hosting is to cPanel Inc.'s own forum, `http://forums.cpanel.net/`. In the Ads and Offers area (`http://forums.cpanel.net/forumdisplay.php?f=22`) there are a number of web hosts who post specials.

Once you've tracked down a few hosts that offer plans you are interested in you'll want to find a site where you can compare those hosts to find the best one for your needs. One such site is `http://findmyhosting.com/`. Here you will find articles on a number of web hosting-related topics as well as an extensive database comparing many hosts and their hosting plans. Not only can you find hosting plans based on how much you are willing to pay, but you can also search based on a wide variety of other criteria such as where the web host is located, the standard features they offer and even how well actual customers rate them. Although most sites like this do not allow you to search based on the type of hosting control software used, if you already have a short list of possibilities, you can compare these hosts to fine-tune your selection.

The Quest for Features

Many hosts offer a plethora of features with their hosting plans and it can be quite confusing to figure out what you really need. Here are some of the most important features you should look for in any web hosting plan:

- **Disk Space**: This is a measure of how much *stuff* you can store on the server. Disk space is measured in either *computer* megabytes, (1 MB = 1,024 KB) or metric standard gigabytes, (1 GB = 1,000 MB). If you are unsure how disk space is measured, you should ask the host. How much space you actually need depends on what you plan to do with your website. If your site is going to be just a few static web pages that won't change often, then you could probably do with as little as 20 MB of disk space. If you plan on creating an online photo gallery, expect to need a lot more disk space, several GB, typically (pictures and media files tend to take up a lot of space). Generally most people seem to think they need far more disk space than they really do. The key is to get a bit more than you think you will use right now, but not too much more. When in doubt, assume you will use less disk space than you think you need.

- **Bandwidth**: Bandwidth is a measure of how much data is transferred to or from your hosting account. Typically this is measured in computer gigabytes. Again, if you are unsure about how your host measures bandwidth, be sure to ask. Bandwidth includes any and all traffic coming to or from the server for your domain including web pages, FTP transfers, e-mail, and so on. Bandwidth on most cPanel servers is measured from the beginning of one calendar month to the beginning of the next. Bandwidth is typically reset some time on the first of every month. People tend to use more bandwidth than they think they need, so getting more is always a good thing. Many hosting companies make obtaining extra bandwidth rather expensive (sometimes as much as $5 per extra GB over the standard plan amount), so generally it is better to upgrade to the next higher hosting plan rather than pay for extra bandwidth every month.

- **MySQL Databases**: Databases are used to store information. Even though you may never have used a database before, you will need at least one for web hosting. The reason for this is that many web-based programs (typically called scripts) use a database to store data that gets accessed regularly. For example, many forums and photo gallery scripts require the use of a database. While you can often get away with just one if your needs are modest, you should ideally look for plans with *unlimited* databases so you can feel free to use as many as you need. Keep in mind that data stored in databases typically counts against your disk space usage, so while you may be able to create as many databases as you want, you still cannot go over the total disk space assigned to your hosting plan.

- **PHP**: PHP is a programming language that a lot of web-based scripts use. Make sure any host you choose offers at least PHP 4.4.1 or later.

PHP rather unimaginatively stands for PHP: Hypertext Preprocessor. PHP 5 is the latest major version of PHP but not all PHP scripts work well with PHP 5 at the time of writing (because PHP 5 is fairly new). PHP 4.4.x offers the widest compatibility. You should avoid any web host that offers PHP 4.3.x or earlier as these versions contain some potentially serious security issues.

Questions to Ask Hosting Companies

Once you have two or three companies on your hosting short list, you need to contact each one of them and ask plenty of questions. This cannot be stressed enough: if you want to really be sure you've picked the right host, you need to ask questions before you sign up. If you don't do that you could be unpleasantly surprised later.

Here is a sample list of questions (along with hints about what sort of answers you should get) that you may wish to ask a potential host.

How's the Company's Support?

There are lots of companies out there offering all sorts of features trying to compete for your money, but the most important feature is support. Tons of features don't mean a thing if your host is missing in action when your website goes down.

- **Do you have true 24/7 technical support?** Some companies claim they have this, but when you actually try to get support you might find that help at 2 AM is rather sparse. If you can submit your questions late at night, this is a good test to see if they are serious about their claims.

- **What support methods do you offer?** Phone, fax, e-mail, helpdesk ticket, live help, instant messenger, etc. It is always good to know what alternative contacts are available in the case of a serious emergency. Always try to respect a web host's *chain of support* though. If they want most of their support requests to come in via e-mail, don't pick up the phone and call them every time you have a question or minor issue.

- **Do you have any guaranteed response time for support requests?** Most hosts will *not* have a guaranteed response time, but the response time should be reasonably short. If you are paying 40 USD a year for hosting it may not be reasonable to expect responses in 15 minutes or less, but answers in less than an hour for critical items and less than 6 hours for less serious support requests is a good thumb rule.

What Special Features does the Company Offer?

Many companies offer special perks with their service. You should be sure that you understand these perks before signing up or you may find that that special feature your host offers isn't nearly as *special* as you had hoped.

- **Do you provide free domain names with your hosting accounts?** A domain name is typically required for web hosting so people can find your site. Some hosts offer free domain names when you buy web hosting from them. Be careful, though, as some hosts will keep your domain name if you decide to leave them, causing major headaches for you if you've spent much time promoting that domain. Domain registrars like GoDaddy, http://godaddy.com/ offer inexpensive domain registration, so if you have any doubt about your host's policies you should register your own domain and not use the offered free domain.

- **Do you offer a referral program?** Some hosts offer special gifts or free hosting if you refer friends or family to them. Be sure you know what they offer so you don't miss out on free stuff if you like the host.

- **Do you automatically back up data on all servers in case of an emergency?** Please note that regardless of your host's answer to this question you should always make your own regular backups. Thanks to Murphy's Law, the one time you don't have a backup is the time that your host's backup drive will fail also.

What are the Company's Hosting Policies?

Amid all of the marketing material on your potential host's website there is usually some *fine print* (or worse yet, some things aren't even mentioned publicly) concerning the rules they impose on themselves and customers. You need to make sure the host's rules don't interfere with your current and future plans for your website.

- **What sort of hardware do you use for your servers?** Ideally, fast dual processors and at least 2 GB of RAM are what you are looking for.

- **How many accounts do you generally place on a shared hosting server before you consider it full?** Many hosts won't be able to quote an exact number, but you are looking for an honest ballpark figure. If they tell you they don't put more than 10 accounts on a shared server and you see their average account costs about $5 a month then clearly the host isn't telling you the truth. A ballpark figure of 100-200 accounts per server on fast hardware is OK. If they use single Celeron CPU servers with 512 MB of RAM, then 20-30 accounts would be OK.

- **Do you offer a money-back guarantee?** If so, how long do I have before the guarantee expires? A good host should have at least a 14-day money-back guarantee so if you find that this host isn't the right one for your needs you can move on to another host without wasting money. Ideally, they should offer a full 1-month guarantee.

- **If I pre-pay for a year and then need to cancel my account half-way through the year, how do you handle that? What if I want to upgrade my plan in the middle of this term?** Many hosts offer a discount if you pre-pay for a full year of service in advance. The host should always offer to refund any full months of unused service on a pro-rated basis. An example of a pro-rated refund: You buy a year of hosting for 100 USD and have used 3 months and cancel your account, the host should give you back approximately 75 USD (100 USD minus three months of service at 8.33 USD a month, 75.01 USD). Note that not all hosts offer pro-rated refunds (or even offer refunds at all). Hosts can handle upgrades in several ways, but always be sure you are getting your money's worth.

- **Do you have any uptime guarantee?** If so, how does the guarantee work? Many hosts claim to offer 99.9% or greater uptime, but you may find that a host can't live up to that promise. If your site is unavailable for more than approximately 44 minutes in a given month through no fault of your own you may be due some recompense. You should find out what your host will do in such cases. Make a note of any limitations on the guarantee. For example, your host might only guarantee the data center in which the server is located will be up 99.9% each month and *not* your particular server. If you have a good host they will always try to *make things right* for their clients after an excessive amount of unplanned downtime without being prodded. Since the host has a business to run don't expect a free month of hosting every time your site is only available 99.8% that month, but they should always offer some sort of recompense.

- **What happens if I use more bandwidth than my plan allows?** cPanel hosts should tell you that your account will be suspended if you go over your bandwidth limit until you either buy extra bandwidth or the first of the next calendar month rolls around. *Do not* buy hosting from any company that says they automatically charge your credit card for every extra GB of bandwidth you use. While this might seem like a nice feature, it is very dangerous. All it takes is a mention of your website on another major site or in the news and you could find yourself with a bandwidth bill of thousands of dollars.

- **What sort of content do you allow on your servers?** Some hosts do not allow certain kinds of content on their servers and you should know what the restrictions are before you sign up. Some hosts do not allow adult hosting or IRC servers, for example. Further, some place restrictions on the types of media you can host. If you want to host your band's website and your host does not permit hosting of music or video files, you may want to look elsewhere.

If your potential web host answers too many questions in an unsatisfactory way, you probably should move on to evaluating the next host on your list. It is important to always be sure to look for and read the Terms of Service or Acceptable Use policies of any host you are interested in. If you cannot find these legal documents be sure to ask about them. These items may be dry or a difficult read but failing to read them can lead to nasty surprises later.

Summary

In this chapter you learned what cPanel is and what tools you need to work with it. In addition you learned how to search for cPanel hosting companies, what to look for, and what to ask those companies so you can find a perfect host for your needs.

In Chapter 2, you will learn how to access your new cPanel hosting account and begin to explore the interface.

2

Getting Started with cPanel

Now that you have a shiny new cPanel web hosting account, it is time to learn the ropes of cPanel's interface. However, before we can dive into that, we need to figure out how to access the account.

Logging into cPanel

Once you've signed up for a web hosting account you will likely receive an e-mail with important account information. Please follow the directions you receive and do not delete that information; you may need to refer to it again some day.

If you are ready to start exploring cPanel, launch your web browser. There are two ways you can log into your cPanel account:

- **Securely (recommended)**: `https://domain.com:2083/` or `https://111.111.111.111:2083/`. If you log in securely you will probably receive a warning about the security certificate not matching. This is normal in this case. Accept the certificate and continue with logging in.

- **Insecurely (non-encrypted connection)**: `http://domain.com:2082/` or `http://domain.com/cpanel` or `http://111.111.111.111:2082/`. Although using this method probably won't display a warning message, let me warn you that the first method is safer and less prone to interference. Use it if you can.

Any time you see *domain.com* in this book, replace it with **your domain name** and replace *111.111.111.111* with the **IP address of the server** that your account is on. It is likely that the server IP address was in the e-mail you received with your account information.

You will be asked for your username and password (which was probably included in the e-mail you received with your hosting account details). If you are unsure what your username and password are, contact your web host.

Logging into cPanel from Behind a Firewall

For security reasons, it is recommended that you do not try to log into your cPanel account from a public location such as a library, school, or office. However, there may be times when you have to log into your account but for some reason the standard login methods mentioned above do not work. Often this is because the location from which you are trying to connect does not allow these sorts of special connections. If so, all is not lost. It may still be possible to connect to cPanel. http://cpanelproxy.net/ offers some software called a proxy that can sometimes allow connections to cPanel even if normal access is blocked.

> Please check with your host before attempting to install this or any proxy software. Many web hosts do not allow proxies to be used.

The cPanel proxy can be installed manually into your account, but there are no online directions and making any mistakes can cause your account to becoming at least partially inaccessible. If you want to have the cPanel proxy installed manually, you should contact your web host and ask them to install it for you (there may be a charge for this).

A much simpler (but less secure) way of installing the cPanel proxy is using the web-based auto-installer. This auto-installer requires that you enter your cPanel account username and password into a form. To be safe you should always change your cPanel password immediately after installing this proxy software.

To use the auto-installer, visit http://cpanelproxy.net/autoinstall and fill out the short form. Enter your cPanel account username and then password. The form then asks for the *server*. This can be the IP address of your server (check the account information you were sent when you signed up for the web hosting service) or the actual name of the server (ask your web host) or even your domain name (domain.com) if it is working. Next, there are three checkboxes: Webmail, cPanel, and WHM. Webmail will allow you to log into your cPanel web mail clients (see Chapter 4) from behind a firewall. cPanel is your cPanel account itself and WHM is something that only those with reseller web hosting accounts have access to. The first two will be checked by default. Leave the checkboxes as they are and then click Install to start the installation. If you entered all the information correctly, you will be told that the proxy was installed for webmail and cPanel. If you see any errors, please double-check the information you entered in the form.

Once the cPanel proxy is installed, you can access your cPanel account from http://cpanel.domain.com/ and log in with your cPanel username and password as you normally would.

> While the cPanel proxy generally works well, it will slow down your connection to cPanel noticeably and some cPanel features might not work as expected. If you find you are having problems doing something in cPanel be sure to log out and log back into cPanel normally without the proxy and see if the problem you are experiencing goes away. Also it is not possible to use the cPanel proxy with a secure (https://) connection.

The Main cPanel Interface

If you have successfully logged into your account, you should be presented with the main cPanel interface, shown below:

Your web host may offer more or fewer features than you see in the screenshot. Also, it is possible that your web host uses a different cPanel theme. To see some other cPanel themes, please turn to Chapter 12.

At the extreme top right side of the cPanel interface you will see two links, HOME and LOGOUT. Clicking HOME will bring you back to this main cPanel screen from wherever you are and clicking LOGOUT will end your session in cPanel.

At the top of the screen you will find information about your web hosting account. You are welcomed to your domain (domain.com) and next to that there is the IP address of the last person that last logged into your cPanel account (if this is your first time logging in you should see None Recorded as shown in the previous figure). The IP address display may help you figure out if your account has been compromised or accessed without your permission. If you see an IP address you don't recognize, you may wish to contact your web host to have them investigate (but please be sure the IP address isn't yours first).

> When someone logs onto your cPanel account using SSL (https://) or via the cPanel proxy, the IP address displayed will be 127.0.0.1.

Under the last login information is a place to change your cPanel account contact address. You can change this as needed by clicking on the word here near where the e-mail address is listed. It is very important that you put a valid e-mail address into this contact area or the server will not be able to contact you if your site is near its bandwidth or disk space limits. Also, your web host might have difficulty contacting you if there are any issues.

General Account Information

To the left side of this screen is a column with a lot of information about the features of your hosting account and the web server your account is located on. From top to bottom:

Hosting Package: This is the hosting plan (or package) that your account is assigned to. It will probably match the name of the hosting plan you signed up for. A hosting plan or package is a collection of features and server resources that you have access to.

Shared/Dedicated IP: The IP address listed here is the one that your website and cPanel account are accessible on. Most likely the IP address is shared with most of the other accounts on this web server. Some hosts will allow you to purchase a dedicated IP address (one used only for your domain). Typically, the only time you would need a dedicated IP address for a domain is if you have purchased an SSL certificate (see Chapter 10 for information on SSL certificates).

Subdomains: This item will list the number of subdomains you currently have created and the maximum your account is allowed. Subdomains are prefixed to the main domain like this, subdomain.domain.com. Subdomains are mostly used to make some part of your website easier to get to or to give a more polished appearance. For example, instead of having visitors go to http://domain.com/store/index.html, you can create a subdomain so that users can visit the easier to remember URL http://store.domain.com/

Parked Domains: Parked domains are other domains you own that are currently pointing to your main domain. Parked domains mirror your main domain's content. For example, if you park seconddomain.com at your account where domain.com is your main domain name, then any time visitors go to seconddomain.com they will see the same content as domain.com. This is a nice feature if you own an extra domain name but do not want to have a separate website for it.

Add-on Domains: These are similar to parked domains, except that an add-on domain creates a special set of directories in your main web account so that your add-on domain gets treated as if it were separate from your main domain. For example, seconddomain.com would have completely separate content from domain.com. This is great if you own more than one domain name and you want to have different content for each site. Add-on domains still count towards your main account's disk space and bandwidth limitations.

Resource Usage

Here you can keep an eye on the various resources your account is using:

Databases: This shows the current and maximum number of MySQL (or PostgreSQL) databases in your account. Many PHP and CGI scripts require the use of at least one MySQL database to work properly.

Disk Usage: This is how much disk space on the server your account is using for *all* features and options. Keep an eye on this to make sure you don't go over your maximum allowed disk space. If you keep your contact e-mail address up to date in cPanel, you will receive an e-mail before you run out of disk space so you can free up room or contact support for additional disk space.

MySQL Disk Usage: This shows how much disk space your MySQL databases are currently using by themselves. This number is included in the disk usage number.

Disk Space Available: This item displays how much of your allowed disk space on the web server you currently have available for use.

Bandwidth Usage: cPanel keeps track of all traffic to and from your account. Watch this number to make sure you don't get too close to your account bandwidth limits in any given month. Typically, bandwidth counters are reset at the beginning of every calendar month, regardless of when your hosting plan billing date is. If you have any questions about how bandwidth is calculated you should contact you web host.

Mail and FTP Information

In this section, you can see quick stats concerning e-mail and FTP:

E-mail Accounts: How many e-mail accounts you have created versus how many you are allowed to have. The first e-mail address in your account will be yourcpanelusername@domain.com and this doesn't count against your maximum number of e-mail accounts allowed. This main e-mail account also cannot be deleted or renamed. Every e-mail account you create uses disk space on your server and contributes to the total amount of disk space you are using for your account.

Forwarders: This item will show you how many e-mail forwarders you currently have set up. You can think of forwarders as *e-mail aliases*. They are e-mail addresses you create (aliasname@domain.com) that aren't full e-mail accounts that can send and receive e-mail.

Forwarders do just that—forward any mail sent to the forwarding address to a different e-mail address (or multiple addresses).

> You can forward mail from your domain to any e-mail address, even if you don't own the domain you are forwarding e-mail to.

Auto-Responders: The number of auto-responders you have set up will be shown here. Auto-responders are special rules you set up so that whenever someone sends an e-mail to a specified e-mail address or that matches certain other criteria, a response is automatically sent with a bit of canned (prepared) text. This feature can be used to set up *on vacation* or *out-of-the-office* auto responses. You can also use auto-responders to send directions or other common information to someone automatically when they send you an e-mail.

Mailing Lists: This item lists the current number of active mailing lists versus the total number you are allowed to have. If you want to send out regular updates, newsletters, or special offers to a large group of people via e-mail, then a mailing list is what you need. cPanel includes special mailing list software called, appropriately, **Mailman**, http://list.org/. See Chapter 4 for more information about mailing lists.

E-mail Filters: Here you see the number of e-mail filters you have set up. E-mail filters can help to block SPAM or keep unwanted messages from getting delivered to any e-mail account. Filters can also help sort e-mails into different locations or mark them based on certain criteria you set.

FTP Accounts: The number of File Transfer Protocol accounts you currently have set up versus the maximum you can have will be shown here. FTP is a method of transferring files from your computer to or from your server. You will probably use FTP to upload web pages to your hosting account.

General Server Information

This is followed by information about the server your account is on:

Operating System: This is the operating system that the server your account is on is running. Probably this will be Linux.

Server Status: Clicking this link will tell you if all of the web server's various features are up and running OK. Green is good, yellow means a service is busy or nearly full (in the case of partition disk space) and red means that service is either very busy, full, or down right now.

pop	up ⬤
named	up ⬤
exim-26	up ⬤
exim (exim-4.52-7_cpanel_smtpctl_av_rewrite_mm2_mmmtrap_exiscan_md5pass)	up ⬤
mysql (4.1.13-standard)	up ⬤
eximstats	up ⬤
spamd	up ⬤
cpsrvd	up ⬤
ftpd	up ⬤
antirelayd	up ⬤
imap	up ⬤
syslogd	up ⬤
httpd (1.3.33 (Unix))	up ⬤
Server Load	0.09 (4 cpus) ⬤
Memory Used	41 % ⬤
Swap Used	0.00 % ⬤
Disk sda5 (/)	13 % ⬤
Disk sda1 (/boot)	7 % ⬤
Disk sda3 (/tmp)	2 % ⬤
Disk sdb1 (/backup)	14 % ⬤

Kernel Version: This is the version of the core of the operating system. This way you can monitor the server to make sure it has all the latest security patches, and so on.

Machine Type: This is the type of processor(s) your server uses. For example, i686 is an Intel brand processor (as opposed to an AMD processor).

Apache Version: This is the version of the web page serving software that is running.

Programming Language and Database Information

If you use any scripts on your website, this section has some important information concerning the programming languages and databases installed on the server:

Perl Version: This is the version of Perl programming language that is currently installed on the server.

Path to Perl: This lists the path to Perl on your server, needed for some Perl scripts.

Path to Sendmail: This is where sendmail, the process that handles sending mail is.

Perl Modules: Perl's functionality can be enhanced by various modules. If you click this link you can see exactly what modules are currently installed.

PHP Version: This is the version of the PHP programming language that is currently installed on the server.

MySQL Version: This is the version of MySQL database software that is currently installed.

cPanel Information

Finally, here we have some information about cPanel itself:

cPanel Build: Every time the developers modify cPanel a new *build* (minor version) is created. New builds may fix bugs, add new features, or improve reliability.

cPanel Theme: This is how the cPanel interface will look. Different themes not only give cPanel a new look, but may also add or remove features. The screenshots in this book show the XSkin theme. You can see what some other themes look like in Chapter 12.

Documentation: Click the link you see here to view a copy of the cPanel documentation maintained by cPanel Inc.

cPanel Pro: Not all web hosts offer cPanel Pro. cPanel Pro allows third-party developers to add new features to cPanel. cPanel has a few sample features that demonstrate what cPanel Pro is capable of. Any items that have icons with a gray background are cPanel Pro features.

Summary

In this chapter you have learned some basic things about the cPanel software:

- How to access cPanel in several different ways
- The main cPanel interface
- Some of the features of your cPanel account

In the next chapter we will discover ways of transferring data to and from your web hosting account.

3

FTP and cPanel's File Manager

It is most likely that one of the first things you will want to do after getting your web hosting account, and taking a quick look at cPanel's interface, is get some files onto your website. So how do you accomplish this? The most common method is via something called FTP. If you have ever downloaded anything on the Internet before, you have likely used FTP, perhaps without even realizing it. FTP stands for File Transfer Protocol. It is a method of transferring files from remote locations to your local computer (called downloading) and vice versa (sending files from your computer to a remote location is called uploading).

In this chapter we will cover most methods that cPanel provides to enable you to transfer files to and from your web hosting account, including:

- Discussing methods of uploading files to your hosting account
- Learning about the types of FTP clients available
- Learning how to work with FTP
- Accessing the main FTP account
- Creating FTP accounts and placing limits on those accounts
- Deleting FTP accounts
- Checking FTP quotas for accounts you create
- Managing Anonymous FTP access
- Monitoring FTP access and killing FTP sessions
- SFTP (Secure FTP)
- FXP (File Exchange Protocol)
- Navigating your site with the cPanel file manager
- Uploading files and downloading files, editing and managing files with the file manager
- WYSIWYG HTML editing via WYSIWYG Pro in the file manager

Before discussing FTP and other file transfer methods in cPanel, we need to learn a bit more about the various types of FTP tools that you can use.

FTP Basics

For those of you who may not be familiar with FTP, it is important to understand what FTP is, what it does, and what sorts of tools you need to use it.

General FTP Tools

There are many tools that can handle FTP in one form or another, but not all are created equal for our purposes. These can be broadly categorized as:

- **Web Browsers**: Although most web browsers can handle FTP, they generally only handle it in a single direction (remote files to local computer) and they cannot handle the reverse (local files to remote computer) or do not handle it well. It is not recommended that you use a web browser to handle FTP to or from your website.

- **HTML/Website Editing Programs**: If you use any sort of website editor that runs off of your computer (like Macromedia Dreamweaver, Adobe GoLive, Nvu, and so on), it most likely has the ability to upload, download, and synchronize files via FTP. The focus of these sorts of programs is to create web content and the ability to FTP files to your web hosting account is just a convenience. If you plan to only work on your website in one of these sorts of programs, then the FTP features should serve you well.

- **Stand-alone FTP Clients**: This category includes all programs that are designed primarily to work with FTP, though they may handle other types of transfers as well. It is recommended that you download and install one of these types of programs even if you have only one of the types of items mentioned above. If you plan to do a lot of work with your website, you might want to try a number of the FTP clients listed in Chapter 13 to see which ones you like best.

Configuring your FTP Client for use with your Main FTP Account

Once you've chosen a program to FTP files to your web hosting account, you should attempt to set it up and test uploading and downloading a file or two to make sure it is working properly. Every cPanel account comes with at least one FTP account, though depending on your hosting plan you may be able to create others. The main FTP account cannot be deleted. To connect to your website via FTP using this main account, you will typically need to provide the following information:

- **FTP Host/Address**: This typically is your domain name with ftp. added to it (ftp.domain.com). You can also use your web server's IP address if your domain name isn't working for some reason.

- **FTP Username**: For the main FTP account this is the same as your cPanel username (8 characters or less).

- **FTP Password**: For the main FTP account this is the same as your cPanel password.

Normally, this is all the information you must enter to access your account via FTP, but some clients may ask for more:

- **Port**: A port is a channel of communication. FTP transfers normally use port 21, although your web host might set it to something else. Always try port 21 first before trying another port.

- **Starting directory**: Typically you won't need to specify this unless you want to start in a different location. This path is a list of directories separated by slashes / (for example `public_html/forum` will start you in the forum directory of your web hosting account, which is inside the `public_html` (web files) directory). Some FTP clients require the starting directory to end with a trailing slash / and some do not. Consult your FTP client program documentation to learn more.

> On Linux servers, folders are called directories.

- **Passive FTP**: There are two primary kinds of FTP connections, active and passive FTP. Passive FTP is a method of sending and receiving FTP information that works well if you are behind a firewall. Generally, you should use passive FTP for all connections since active FTP may get filtered by your ISP or your home firewall. If you'd like more information about the difference between the two types of connections, please visit `http://slacksite.com/other/ftp.html`.

- **Directory Synchronization**: If you are using a web content editor to FTP files you may be asked to specify which directory on your local computer should match with your remote web directory. For example, you may want the contents of `Documents/ website/mydomain/` on your computer to be what people see on your website, so you would set the remote directory to `public_html`. Please see the documentation for your web content editor for more information about this feature if you want to use it.

If you enter the connection information into your FTP client and you are able to upload a test file and download it successfully then you are ready to begin working on your website. If you receive an error message, please check to see that you entered your account information correctly. You may also want to consult the account information you were sent by your web hosting company. If you have a hardware or software firewall or router in the location where you are trying to connect, you should check its settings to make sure it can send and receive through port 21. If it still doesn't work, please contact your web host for assistance.

> On most cPanel web servers, the FTP server has a maximum display limit of 2,000 files per directory. This means that if you have 2,500 files stored in a single directory on the web server you will only be able to see the first 2,000. This limit is designed to help keep the FTP server from crashing or overloading the entire server. It is recommended that you never have more than 2,000 files in any directory, because even if your web host has raised the maximum file limit, working with so many files will slow down your FTP transfers to and from that directory. If you must have more than 2,000 files in a single directory, please contact your web host and see if they are willing to raise that limit.

Creating and Managing FTP Accounts in cPanel

Depending on your hosting plan, you may not be limited to just a single main FTP account. Why would you need more than one? You probably don't if you are the only person who will ever make changes to your website. However, if you have another person or group of people help you edit your website, you shouldn't give them access to your main FTP account to edit files.

> Security Note: Because the main FTP account login is the same as your cPanel login you should never give it to anyone else. If someone needs FTP access to your account, you can create a separate FTP account for him or her unless your hosting plan does not allow it.

If you would like to create or manage additional FTP accounts in cPanel, you should log into your cPanel account and then click on the FTP Manager icon. Then from the menu of options that appear, select FTP Accounts.

FTP Manager

» FTP Accounts
With the FTP account utility you can control FTP accounts for your users or if your account has sub-domain support you can add FTP accounts for your sub-domain(s).

» Setup Anonymous FTP Access
Here you can change how anonymous FTP users should be treated and change the anonymous upload policy as well.

» Anonymous FTP Message
You can edit the anonymous FTP welcome message that users will see when they login to your FTP site.

» FTP Session Control
This utility allows you to disconnect users or time out FTP sessions.

There will probably already be two or more FTP accounts listed here as main account. You can't delete or edit them (although you may be able to edit the disk space quota for some of them). They were created by cPanel automatically and need to remain as they are.

Creating a New FTP Account in cPanel

If you would like to create a new FTP account, follow these basic steps:

1. Click Add Account.
2. Choose a name for the new user and enter it in the Login text box. The directory path will automatically update to match your user's login name. The FTP user you create will *only* have access to the specified directory inside your public_html directory and any directories below that. This starting directory is often referred to as the FTP account's home directory. If you change the directory to / then the FTP user will

have complete access to any files and directories in public_html (your public web space) via FTP. The account won't be able to access any files or directories above the public_html directory. The directions printed at the bottom of the screen make this all fairly clear.

3. When you create an account, you can also specify a disk space quota. The quota limit will restrict the account from uploading more than the specified amount (in MB). Setting the quota limit to nothing, zero (0) or the word *unlimited* will create an FTP account with no quota limits at all. Without a quota limit, that user will be able to upload files until you either run out of disk space or bandwidth.

Add FTP Account

Login: admin2
Password: thisisthepassword941
Quota   unlimited
Directory: /home/domain/public_html /admin2

(Create)   (Clear)

Directions:
If you enter a single / in the directory box, the new FTP user will have access to the entire public_html directory and all directories under it. If you just want the new user to be able to access a sub-domain, just set the directory box to the same value as the sub-domain's root name, which is listed in parenthesis on the sub-domain section of this control panel.

Please be aware that the new user will have read/write access to the directory you choose and every directory below it. For example, if you choose to add the user john, and give the user access to/home/domain/public_html/john directory, the user will be able to add, edit, rename and remove any file or directory in/home/domain/public_html/john.

Once you create an FTP account, you can't edit it (other than the disk space quota). You can only delete it, so type carefully.

A couple of examples of FTP account creation:

You create a new FTP user called billy and the specified home directory is /home/domain/public_html/billy with a disk quota of 10 MB. This user will be able to create or access anything inside the billy directory in your account's public web space area (public_html) via FTP. Billy will only be able to upload 10 MB worth of files into public_html/billy. After uploading that much they will need to delete some files to make room to upload more. The billy FTP account will not be able to access anything in public_html itself.

You also create a new FTP account called webmaster and the home directory is /home/domain/public_html/ with quota set to unlimited. This user will be able to access everything in public_html via FTP and upload/download/delete files and directories with no limits.

For FTP accounts that you create, the username to log into the FTP server is username@domain.com. The password is whatever you set it to (for security the password should not be the same as your main FTP account). Otherwise, all of the connection information mentioned for the main FTP account remains the same.

Monitoring your FTP Usage in cPanel

Back at the main FTP Account screen you will be able to monitor FTP account quotas, edit those quotas, and delete FTP accounts that you have previously added.

Rather oddly, there is a link for each add-on domain and sub-domain's raw web logs here (see Chapter 7 for more information on web logs). Click a link and your browser will download the logs to your computer.

Depending on your web host's settings, the raw web log links may include your main FTP/cPanel account password as well as the username. While this makes accessing the links easy (since you do not have to enter the password for your account to access the raw web logs), it is also a security risk. If you leave this page open in your browser anyone can come along and roll the mouse pointer over the link to see your main account username and password in the browser status bar. You may want to ask your web host to turn off the option that includes account passwords in those links.

Anonymous FTP Access

From the FTP Manager screen you can also set up or control anonymous FTP access. Anonymous FTP allows people without FTP accounts to access a special public_ftp directory to upload or download files.

Anonymous FTP access (especially anonymous FTP uploads) can be a big security risk, so your web host may not permit you to turn this feature on. If anonymous FTP access is turned off on your web server, accessing any of cPanel's anonymous FTP options won't affect anything. You should contact your web host if you want to know if they support anonymous FTP access.

To turn anonymous FTP access on or off, you should click Setup Anonymous FTP Access from the FTP Manager screen in cPanel. You will be presented with two simple checkboxes. The first allows you to offer anonymous (public) FTP access to ftp.domain.com (only the public_ftp directory). The next checkbox allows anonymous (public) FTP upload access to your ftp.domain.com/public_ftp/incoming/ directory. Both of these items should be unchecked for security reasons unless you are certain you want to offer anonymous FTP access.

Please note that to offer complete anonymous FTP access (especially uploads), your account may need to be assigned a dedicated IP address.

Anonymous FTP Welcome Message

Enter the message your visitors will see when they connect to your anonymous FTP server:

Welcome to my server, please behave or you will be banished. :)

(Save Message)

If you want people logging in via anonymous FTP to see a custom message from you when they log into your server, then write it here. This will only get displayed if the FTP client the person is using displays messages from the server. Some web browsers will display this message when accessing your account via FTP, but many people turn off viewing such messages especially if they are using a dedicated FTP program. In most cases, if the message is not displayed on screen, it is still written to the user's FTP transcript (log).

cPanel FTP Session Control

Here you can see anyone who is currently logged into your FTP site and choose to kick them off the server. The session information shows this information (in order): type of FTP service running, what they are doing now, and the time they started this session. Click the word Disconnect next to the logon time to end that user's session immediately.

FTP Session Control

Session	Login time	
pure-ftpd (IDLE)	01:03	Disconnect
pure-ftpd (DOWNLOAD)	01:07	Disconnect

Other Types of FTP Connections

FTP has more tricks up its sleeve than just active or passive connections. It is also possible to connect securely to an FTP site and also perform direct remote to remote server file transfers.

Secure FTP

Secure FTP (also known as SFTP) is a more secure method of transferring and working with files. It encrypts all traffic to and from your web server so no one else can access your data, similar to SSL (`https://`) access of web pages in a browser, but for file transfers. SFTP is actually a combination of two different protocols, **SSH (Secure Shell**—see Chapter 10 for information on SSH) and standard FTP. In order to access your account via SFTP, you will need three things:

- The main FTP account
- SSH (regular or jailshell) access to your account
- An FTP client that supports SFTP (most dedicated clients will)

> You may need to contact your web host to get SSH access for your cPanel account.

Accessing your account via SFTP is simple if your FTP client supports it; you use the main FTP account login details as you normally would, but you tell your FTP client to try to access the account via SFTP.

> SFTP uses port 22, the standard port for SSH access, so make sure if you use a firewall that port 22 is open.

FXP Transfers

FXP stands for File eXchange Protocol. FXP is FTP directly between two separate FTP accounts you are logged into via your FTP client. FXP allows you to transfer files directly from one remote server to another one without having to download the files to your local computer first. Not only does it save a step, but FXP transfers are often much faster than uploads and downloads to your computer since the two servers communicate directly with each other using your account login on both servers. Some servers also support SFTP FXP transfers.

FXP requires all of the following in order to work:

- Valid FTP/SFTP accounts on both servers you want to transfer files between. It is extremely rare for a server to allow anonymous FXP.
- Both servers must allow FXP. Many do not. If only one of the two servers allows FXP then it will not work.
- An FTP client that supports FXP (and SFTP FXP if you want to use that). This is becoming more common, but many clients still don't support FXP.

If any of those conditions are not met, FXP will fail.

> You should contact your web host if you want to find out if your web server supports FXP.

cPanel's File Manager

FTP is not the only way to manage files and directories in your hosting account. cPanel includes a File Manager that will allow you to do almost anything you can via FTP (and a number of things that cannot be done via FTP) right in your web browser. The cPanel File Manager does have limitations that do not make it an ideal choice if you need to work with lots of files. However, it can come in quite handy at times, especially for quick remote edits without access to an FTP client.

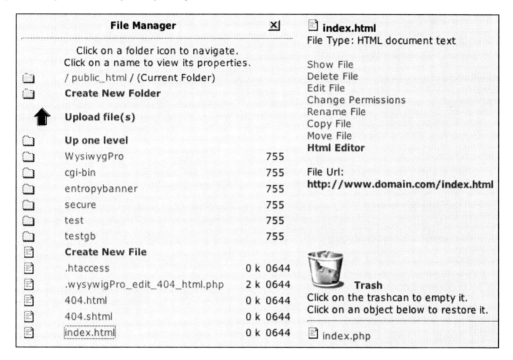

To start using the cPanel File Manager, log into your cPanel account and click the File Manager icon. A new window will open with the File Manager interface. On the left are your site and all files and directories. On the right will appear information about whatever action you are trying to perform.

Clicking on the name of a file or directory on the left will allow you to work with or rename that item. Clicking the small folder icon next to a directory will open that directory and show you the contents, where you can upload, download, or work with files there.

On the right side of the screen is a sidebar where you can perform basic actions on files or directories you select (like view, edit, change permissions, throw them in the site trash, and so on).

A Few Words about File Permissions

If you work with files and directories on a Linux server it is important to understand a bit about permissions. In order to make sure that only those people who are supposed to have access to a directory or file can actually do so, Linux has a file and directory permission system. Every file and directory has permissions set for three kinds of users:

- **User**: The owner or creator of the file or directory
- **Group**: A group of users that are permitted to use a directory or file in some way
- **World**: Everyone else who isn't the owner or creator or a member of the correct group (You can think of *world* as public permissions)

For each kind of user, there are three basic categories of permissions:

- **Read**: Any type of user that is allowed read access can do just that, read a file. If a user only has this permission, they can open the file or directory and see the contents, but they may not make changes.
- **Write**: If the user has write permission, they can make changes to a file and save those changes or in the case of a directory, they can put files and directories inside that directory. It is possible to have write-only access to a directory or file.
- **Execute**: In the case of binary files (code designed to run on Linux), a user with execute access can run that file or items in that directory. Think of this permission as the ability to launch an application (though it is a bit more complex than that).

The most common method of referring to permissions is using a three-digit number. If you work with web applications (scripts) you will often be told to set permissions on files or directories to some three-digit number. The way this works is every type of permission has a certain unique numerical value: Read permission is 4, Write permission is 2 and Execute permission is 1, no permissions at all is 0. These numbers are added together for each kind of user. For example, a user with Read and Write, but not Execute permission is assigned a value of 6. Every type of user has their own numerical value expressed in the order of User, Group, World, for example, 755 (User has Read, Write, and Execute permissions; Group has Read and Execute permissions only and so does World). The maximum number for each kind of user is 7. So 777 is Read, Write, and Execute access for everyone (no restrictions at all). It is much easier to figure out these numerical values by setting up a grid, like cPanel's File Manager does:

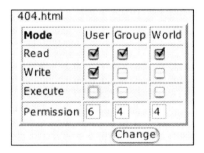

The File Manager does the math for you. All you need to do is to check the various permission categories for each kind of user.

If you want to figure out numerical Linux permissions but don't want to use the cPanel File Manager, you can access an online version of this permissions calculator at `http://wsabstract.com/script/script2/chmodcal.shtml`. This page also offers the code for this web-based calculator so you can add it to your own website if you wish.

How are users and groups defined and assigned? Linux and cPanel handle it automatically. Any files you upload via FTP or the cPanel File Manager will be assigned your main cPanel username as the user and the group. Some web applications create files and directories with the user and group nobody (this is just the name of the user and group, not an indication of who can access it) or your cPanel username for both user and group. You should not need to change a file or directory's assigned user or group, but if you do you should contact your web host to handle it for you.

If you are using a supported browser (Internet Explorer 5+, Mozilla 1.4+, Netscape 7.1+, or Firefox 1.0+) you will be able to edit HTML files in a **WYSIWYG (What-You-See-Is-What-You-Get)** interface similar to many commercial web page editors. The program cPanel uses to edit HTML files is called WYSIWYG Pro. You can learn more about this program and its many features at `http://wysiwygpro.com/`.

If you make a mistake and put something in the trash that you want to get back, just click the name of the directory or file that appears below the trashcan icon. Clicking the trash icon itself will *delete* any directories or files that you have permission to delete that are currently in the site trash. *This action is not undoable*. Make sure you actually delete the files in the trash or they will still count against your disk space limits for your account (because the file is not actually deleted yet). Close this window when you are done and you will be back at your cPanel.

cPanel's File Manager is not really designed for heavy-duty file manipulation (for example it isn't designed to work on more than one item at a time), but it can come in handy if you just need to make a few quick changes and you aren't in a place where you have access to a real FTP client. However, there is one very nice thing about the File Manager—it is logged into your account as a special kind of user, so it can sometimes delete files and directories that you may not be able to delete in your FTP client because you aren't listed as the owner of the file or directory. Be sure to give it a try before contacting your web host for help.

Summary

In this chapter you learned how to create, manage, limit, and remove FTP accounts. You also learned how to use cPanel's own File Manager to upload, download, and manage files and directories in your hosting account.

In the next chapter you will learn how to manage e-mail using cPanel's many tools and features.

4

Working with Mail

You may have initially purchased your web hosting account just to get your site onto the Internet, but depending on the hosting plan you purchased you may also have the ability to create/manage e-mail accounts for your domain. In fact, some web hosts offer inexpensive e-mail-only cPanel accounts that don't include web hosting.

Why Manage your Own E-mail Accounts?

If you already have e-mail accounts from other sources (perhaps through your ISP or from a free service like Hotmail or Gmail) you might be wondering why you should bother with more e-mail accounts. Here are a few of the many reasons:

- **Give your communication a more polished appearance**: This is especially important if you are running your own business. If you sell products online and then ask people to contact you at an AOL or Hotmail e-mail account, they may wonder if your company is real. With e-mail coming from your domain, you can give the impression that you are a large business even if you're just running it out of your basement.

- **Complete control over your e-mail**: You can forward e-mail to one or more people automatically, create or remove extra e-mail addresses whenever you want, forward all mail sent to your domain to another domain altogether. The choice is yours. You are only limited by the disk space and features permitted in your hosting plan.

- **Improved anti-spam features**: You have complete control over the advanced spam fighting technologies cPanel offers. Several of these features are of the sort you find in expensive commercial products, but you get them all for no additional charge (depending on your web host).

- **Wide range of choices concerning how to access your e-mail**: Access your e-mail from any web browser securely, download it to your local computer or manage mail both locally and on the web at the same time.

Although the freedom managing your own e-mail gives you is a wonderful thing, this doesn't mean you should completely abandon all other e-mail addresses. You should keep at least one other e-mail address that isn't part of your hosted domain (even the free e-mail services will do). The reason for this is unless you have a dedicated server, there will be times (exceedingly rare times, it is hoped) when your hosted domain may go down or perhaps you run out of disk space or bandwidth. You do need to have an alternative e-mail address where your web host and other people can get in touch with you if your domain isn't working.

Though at first, you maybe overwhelmed by the profusion of features, managing your own e-mail accounts with cPanel isn't very difficult. Once you've had a chance to experiment with the various options a bit, you'll be managing your e-mail like a pro!

Common E-mail Terms

When discussing e-mail you will be exposed to a number of different terms that you may not be familiar with. Here are the most common:

Bounced E-mail: E-mail messages that get returned to the sender because there was some sort of problem and the e-mail could not be delivered.

E-mail Address: This is what people type in to send e-mail to you—user@domain.com. E-mail addresses always include the @ (at sign).

E-mail Body: The main section of the e-mail with whatever text you have written.

E-mail Headers: Several lines of information that appear prior to the body of an e-mail message. The headers contain a lot of information about where mail has come from and which mail server received it. Most e-mail programs don't show full headers by default since there can be so many of them. If you are having problems with spam or bounced e-mail messages, the full headers of the message contain information that can help track down the problem.

IMAP: This is a protocol for fetching e-mail from a remote web server. IMAP is designed to manage all mail on the remote mail server. IMAP is a good protocol to use if you travel a lot and want to be able to access all of your mail from anywhere. However, if your mail server is having problems you likely won't be able to access any mail (even old mail) until the server comes back online.

Mailbox: The location where mail is stored for an e-mail address.

MX Record: An MX (Mail eXchange) record tells the server where e-mail for a particular domain should be sent.

Password Authentication: This is one method you can use to prove that the e-mail account is yours. You enter your account username and password.

POP3: This is a protocol for fetching e-mail from a mail server. This method was designed to retrieve mail from a remote mail server and store the e-mail locally. Mail fetched via POP3 typically gets removed from a server once your e-mail client has fetched the mail (though you can change this behavior). Since mail is removed from the server, you typically can only read old mail in the e-mail program used to download the messages. If your mail server goes down, you will still be able to access old mail locally without an Internet connection.

POP-Before-SMTP Authentication: An alternative SMTP (send mail) authentication method. To use this method, you must log in to your e-mail account via POP3 and check your e-mail. If you do that successfully then you will be able to send e-mail from that account for 30 minutes via SMTP without having to enter the account username and password again. This is a somewhat less secure than password authentication and not all web hosts support it.

SMTP: Stands for Simple Mail Transfer Protocol. SMTP is the protocol used when you need to send someone e-mail from your account.

Web Mail (Client): A program that allows you to access your e-mail from a web browser.

Accessing cPanel's E-mail Features

Any features that have anything to do with e-mail can be found by clicking the Mail icon on the main cPanel screen.

```
          Mail Manager Main Menu

    >>  Web Mail

    >>  Email Domain Forwarding

    >>  Manage/Add/Remove Accounts

    >   Default Address

    >>  Auto-responders

    >   E-mail Filtering

    >>  Forwarders

    >>  Mailing Lists

    >   SpamAssassin

    >>  BoxTrapper Spam Trap

    >   Trace an E-mail Address

    >>  Modify Mail Exchanger (MX Entry)
```

Managing POP3 and IMAP E-mail Accounts

If you want to create new e-mail accounts or work with existing ones, you should click on Manage/Add/Remove Accounts. This is where you go if you want to set up a POP3/IMAP e-mail account.

Mail Account Maintenance

Address	Login	Disk Used	Quota						
Main Account	domain			Read Webmail	Aging				Configure Mail Client
admin@domain.com	admin@domain.com	0.00 Meg	10.00 Meg	Delete Read Webmail	Aging	Change Quota	Change Pass		Configure Mail Client

Be sure to enable SMTP Authentication in your E-mail client or you may not be able to send mail. If your e-mail client has trouble using a @ sign in the login, you can use +, :, or % sign instead.

[Add Account] | [Go Back]

Every cPanel account comes with one administrator e-mail address by default. This administrator e-mail account matches both your cPanel account username (so the e-mail address is cpanelusername@domain.com) and password. If you change your cPanel account password, the main e-mail account password will change also. You may choose to use this account or not, but this account cannot be deleted.

> There is one advantage to the administrator e-mail account (at the time of writing this book); it has the ability to see mail left for other users. To do that, you need to log into the account via web mail and you should then be able to choose the various mailboxes set up for e-mail accounts in your domain. While you cannot send mail as these users, you can read, forward, respond to (as the administrator) and delete any e-mail in these mailboxes.

Creating an E-mail Account

To create another e-mail account, just click the Add Account button at the bottom of the screen. This will take you to the new e-mail account setup screen. Here you set the username for the e-mail address (username@domain.com), set the password, and choose the mail quota (more commonly referred to as mailbox size) for the account. If you leave the quota blank, then the mailbox can grow until your web hosting account runs out of disk space. If you do set a mailbox size, then that e-mail account will stop accepting mail once it hits the quota until the mailbox is cleaned out to make room for more messages. Once you create the account, it is immediately active.

Configuring your E-mail Client to Use your New Address

Of course, if you go through the trouble of setting up a real e-mail account, then you will probably want to send/receive mail from that account in your favorite e-mail program (Outlook (Express), Eudora, etc.). If you use Outlook or Outlook Express you can just click the Mail Client Configuration link next to the e-mail address you want to set up. This will take you to a screen where you can click on a link to configure either Outlook or Outlook Express with that e-mail account using either the POP3 or IMAP protocols. Otherwise, you will need to set it up manually.

Configuring Mail Client for admin@domain.com

Please select an application:

Auto-Configure Microsoft Outlook® for IMAP Access
Auto-Configure Microsoft Outlook® for POP3 Access
Auto-Configure Microsoft Outlook Express® for IMAP Access
Auto-Configure Microsoft Outlook Express® for POP3 Access

Manual Settings
Mail Server Username: admin+domain.com
Incoming Mail Server: mail.domain.com
Outgoing Mail Server: mail.domain.com **(server requires authentication)**
Supported Incoming Mail Protocols: POP3, POP3S (SSL/TLS), IMAP, IMAPS (SSL/TLS)
Supported Outgoing Mail Protocols: SMTP, SMTPS (SSL/TLS)

For any given domain name:

- **Account/Username**: username@domain.com OR username+domain.com
- **Password**: the password you set up for that account in cPanel.
- **Mail Server**: mail.domain.com
- **SMTP Server**: mail.domain.com
- **SMTP Authentication**: YES or NO. If you set this to YES (preferred) use password SMTP Authentication and use the same username and password as above). If you set this to NO then you *must* check your e-mail via POP3 before trying to send mail or it will fail with an error message telling you that you must check your e-mail first. Not all web hosts support this method of authentication (called POP-Before-SMTP) and it isn't as secure as requiring standard SMTP authentication before sending mail.
- **Return Address**: username@domain.com

Depending on your web host, you may also be able to use SSL secure mail sending (SMTPS) and receiving. You can find out what protocols your web host supports by clicking on Configure Mail Client and looking at the last paragraph of text on that page. That text tells you how to manually configure your e-mail client and what protocols are supported.

Changing Advanced E-mail Options and Monitoring your E-mail Account

You can edit the mail quota at any time for all e-mail accounts you have created. To do that, you should click on the Change Quota link next to the e-mail account you want to edit. Enter the new quota in MB and click on Change to make the new mail quota size active.

Depending on how your web host has the mail server set up, mail that comes in for an account that is over the set quota will either be stored in a temporary queue until enough space is cleared out to allow the message to be delivered (up to 3 days at most before deleting the message) or be deleted immediately without delivering it; so watch mail quotas carefully.

To see how much disk space each account is using (for stored mail), click Show Disk Space Used and the amount of disk space in use and the maximum quota will be displayed next to each e-mail account. Note that the main e-mail account will not show this information.

Clicking on Aging will allow you to set a POP3 aging (mail expiration) time. Usually, if you use POP3 to check your e-mail it gets downloaded to your local computer and then removed off the remote mail server. However it is possible with most e-mail clients to download a local copy of your mail while keeping a copy of that mail on the server. If you keep your mail on the server all the time there is a chance that the account might go over the mail quota and you won't receive more e-mail until you manually clear out some old e-mail. To avoid this, you can automate deletion of old mail that is over a certain number (that you specify) of days old. This is called aging and only works with the POP3 protocol, not web mail or IMAP. If you don't regularly check e-mail via POP3, then the old mail will not get deleted automatically. The default setting for aging is 0 days (which turns the aging feature off).

Another thing you can do from the Manage/Add/Remove Accounts screen is change the password for any account you have created. Click Change Pass next to the e-mail account you want to change it for and then enter the new password. The change will take effect immediately.

Web Mail

It is nice to be able to check mail from your home computer, but what happens if you need to check e-mail from some other location? You can use web mail. Web mail clients allow you to do almost everything you can do with your preferred local e-mail client program, but you can access it from nearly any web browser from anywhere on the Internet.

Accessing Web Mail

There are several ways to access web mail, just as there are several ways to access cPanel. You have your choice of the following:

- `http://domain.com/webmail/`
- `http://domain.com:2095/`
- `https://domain.com:2096/` (secure SSL connection)

All of these connection methods take you to exactly the same web mail management page:

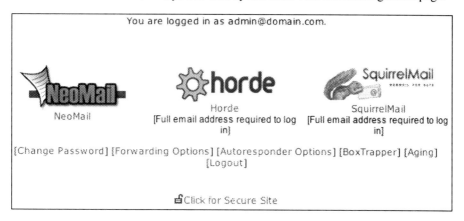

If you have problems accessing web mail using ports 2095 or 2096, you can use cPanel proxy to access web mail as well via the web standard port 80. If you followed my advice in Chapter 1, you already have web mail proxy access set up. If not, please check with your web host to make sure using this proxy is OK and then visit http://cpanelproxy.net/ and use the auto-installer to install it. Once completed, you can also access web mail this way using http://webmail.domain.com/.

> Remember, the cPanel proxy doesn't work with secure (SSL) connections and it will slow down access to web mail to some extent.

From the cPanel web mail management screen, you have access to at most three different web mail clients, **NeoMail**, **Horde**, or **SquirrelMail**.

NeoMail is the simplest and fastest loading web mail client but it is short on features and will be dropped soon from cPanel because it won't work with the **Courier IMAP** server software that cPanel will eventually make standard. (cPanel currently uses uwimap, though your web host may have already switched to Courier. If so, NeoMail won't work.)

SquirrelMail offers a clean interface with the ability to add lots of plug-ins or change the look of the web mail client through use of themes. Please note that the default installation of SquirrelMail in cPanel doesn't include many plug-ins (like a spelling checker, language translation, spam reporting, HTML mail viewing, and so on) unless your web host has enabled them.

Horde is another good web mail client. It includes a calendar, to do list, and memo area as well as a robust e-mail service. The downside is that it is rather complex and some people don't like the interface. I recommend you try both SquirrelMail and Horde and see which you prefer.

You may prefer to set up a subdomain like webmail.domain.com that takes the user directly to your preferred web mail client to log in (see Chapter 6 for more on subdomains).

Direct links to web mail clients in cPanel:

- **NeoMail**: `http://domain.com:2095/NeoMail/NeoMail.pl`
- **Horde**: `http://domain.com:2095/horde/login.php`
- **SquirrelMail**: `http://domain.com:2095/3rdparty/squirrelmail/webmail.php`

In addition to allowing you to choose which web mail program you want to use, the cPanel web mail management screen allows you to edit a number of mail options for this e-mail address including:

- Your e-mail account password
- E-mail forwarding options
- Auto-response options
- BoxTrapper anti-spam features
- POP3 e-mail aging settings

Clicking the lock icon will switch from non-secure to secure (SSL) web mail access.

To check your mail using the main administrator account, you should enter your cPanel username and password. For all other e-mail accounts that you set up for your domain, you should enter the full e-mail address (user@domain.com) and the e-mail password. You can also use + . % , or : in place of the @ sign if you prefer or if your web browser doesn't like @ signs in usernames.

You can also access web mail for each account by clicking the Webmail link next to the e-mail account name you want to check on the mail account maintenance screen. You will be asked for the e-mail account password and then taken to the standard cPanel web mail screen.

E-mail Forwarders (Aliases)

Forwarders are not full e-mail accounts; they just redirect mail to another e-mail address or addresses. For this reason, e-mail forwarders are also sometimes known as e-mail aliases. Forwarders are very useful, particularly if you want to have a number of different e-mail addresses without the hassle of having to check several different accounts. Just create the forwarding e-mail address and point it to your *real* e-mail account of choice. In fact, you can even have e-mail sent to a forwarding address that is redirected to many other recipients. To do this, set up the same forwarding e-mail address with multiple recipients (you can add multiple addresses at one time by separating each with a comma or you can set up each one separately if you prefer). You can use this feature to create simple group e-mail addresses. For example, you can set a forwarding e-mail address that automatically redirects any mail sent to that address to your entire family. This is great for personal announcements or a small mailing list without the hassle of setting up a full-fledged mailing list.

You can send mail so that it looks like it came from an e-mail forwarding account by setting up a new *personality* or account in your e-mail program of choice and setting the name and return e-mail address to your e-mail forwarding address and then using the standard mail/SMTP (send mail) addresses for your preferred *real* e-mail account. For example, to send mail so it looks like it comes from admintwo@domain.com when it is really coming from admin@domain.com:

Display name for e-mail: Administrator2

Return Address: admintwo@domain.com

Incoming Mail Server: mail.domain.com

Outgoing Mail Server: mail.domain.com

Username for POP3 and SMTP Authorization: admin@domain.com

Password for POP3 and SMTP Authorization: password of your *admin* e-mail account

> Some ISPs do not allow sending mail that isn't from your real ISP-provided e-mail address. Also, your web host may not allow clients to send mail via SMTP that isn't from a real e-mail address.

E-mail Domain Forwarding

E-mail domain forwarding is a way to send all e-mail from one domain, subdomain, parked or add-on domain to the same address at a different domain. Select E-mail Domain Forwarding from the mail manager screen and then click Add Domain Forwarder, select the domain to forward and enter the domain name to forward mail to (without www.). You don't have to own or control the domain you want to forward mail *to* (though it must be able to receive mail), but the domain you want to forward mail *from* must be hosted in your account. Once set up, this feature will redirect mail that is supposed to go to user2@domain.com (your cPanel main, sub, add-on, or parked domain) to user2@otherdomain.com (the domain you choose to forward to). So if you have bob@domain.com set up in your cPanel and you have e-mail domain forwarding to otherdomain.com on, the message will be sent to bob@otherdomain.com.

Mailing Lists

Sometimes the basic one-to-many simplicity of forwarding e-mail isn't full-featured enough, especially since it requires a lot of manual entry of e-mail addresses. If you are going to send a newsletter or any regular e-mail to many people, you'll probably want to set up a mailing list. You create one by clicking the Add List button and then filling in the name of the list, the domain name it should come from, and the mailing list administrative password. Then click Create. You will be shown that several files and entries were created to handle this new mailing list. Click Go Back and then click on the Edit List button to finish setting up the mailing list.

Once you enter your mailing list administrative password, you have access to all the features of the Mailman mailing list software. Mailman is very full-featured, but it has so many features that it is beyond the scope of this book. Mailman does have built-in help, which should be enough to answer most of your questions. If you need additional assistance, please check out the documentation at http://list.org/.

Dealing with Unsolicited E-mail (SPAM)

Unsolicited Commercial E-mail (usually referred to as spam or UCE) is a big problem these days and the problem is getting progressively worse as time goes on. If you run a business that relies on e-mail then spam can cost you a lot of money because buried under that avalanche of spam is legitimate e-mail that you have to try and locate. The time you spend dealing with spam is that much less time you have to focus on your customers or clients. How can you cut down on the amount of spam you receive while being careful not to accidentally delete real e-mail? Thankfully, cPanel includes a number of tools that can help you with this task.

SpamAssassin

Spam Assassin can serve as the front-line defense in your anti-spam corpus. It blocks known spammers and rewrites the headers of other e-mail messages so you can filter them out from your e-mail program if you wish. Click the Enable SpamAssassin button to turn it on, then click Configure Spam Assassin to edit the rules that SpamAssassin will use and what exactly it will do to incoming mail.

rewrite_header subject	***SPAM***

Text added to the Subject: line of mails that are considered spam. _HITS_ in the tag will be replace with the calculated score for this message. _REQD_ will be replaced with the threshold.

blacklist_from	
blacklist_from	
blacklist_from	
blacklist_from	
blacklist_from	

Used to specify addresses which send mail that is often tagged (incorrectly) as non-spam, but which the user doesn't want. Same format as whitelist_from.

required_score	5

Set the number of hits required before a mail is considered spam. "n.nn" can be an integer or a real number. 5.0 is the default setting, and is quite aggressive; it would be suitable for a single-user setup, but if you're an ISP installing SpamAssassin, you should probably set the default to be more conservative, like 8.0 or 10.0

score	
score	
score	
score	
score	

Assign scores (the number of points for a hit) to a given test. Scores can be positive or negative real numbers or integers. "SYM-BOLIC_TEST_NAME" is the symbolic name used by SpamAssassin for that test; for example, 'FROM_ENDS_IN_NU'. If only one valid score is listed, then that score is always used for a test. If four valid scores are listed, then the score that is used depends on how SpamAssassin is being used. The first score is used when both Bayes and network tests are disabled. The second score is used when Bayes is disabled, but network tests are enabled. The third score is used when Bayes is enabled and network tests are disabled. The fourth score is used when Bayes is enabled and net-work tests are enabled. Setting a rule's score to 0 will disable that rule from running.

whitelist_from	
whitelist_from	
whitelist_from	
whitelist_from	
whitelist_from	

Used to specify addresses which send mail that is often tagged (incorrectly) as spam; it also helps if they are addresses of big companies with lots of lawyers. This way, if spammers impersonate them, they'll get into big trouble, so it doesn't provide a shortcut around SpamAssassin. Whitelist and blacklist addresses are now file-glob-style patterns, so friend@somewhere.com, *@isp.com, or *.domain.net will all work. Specifically, * and ? are allowed, but all other metacharacters are not. Regular expressions are not used for security reasons.

(Save)

The first 5 lines in the configuration area (blacklist) are reserved for you to add e-mail addresses that you notice SpamAssassin is not marking as spam, but should be. Any mail from these addresses will be automatically marked as spam.

Required_hits affects how aggressive SpamAssassin is in marking messages as spam. A *hit* is when SpamAssassin finds a match in its list of common spam characteristics (out of hundreds of possible matches). The default is 5 hits, which makes SpamAssassin aggressive in labeling messages as spam. Change this to a higher number if you find that messages that are not spam are getting constantly labeled as spam.

The next line, rewrite_subject can be either 0 (zero) or 1. If this is set to zero, as it is by default, SpamAssassin will not change the subject line on any incoming e-mail. If you change this to 1 then SpamAssassin will append whatever you type in the next line subject_tag to the front of the subject of all suspected spam. This will make it easier for you to identify spam and to filter it out of your inbox automatically, should you desire to do so. Note that if you add _HITS_ to the subject_tag line, the actual number of *hits* the suspected spam had will be appended to the subject and if you add _REQD_, the threshold value you set in required_hits will get appended to the subject.

For example, if you change rewrite_subject to 1 and the subject_tag to **Spam** (Had _HITS_ hits, threshold is _REQD_) and you receive a piece of mail that SpamAssassin considers to be spam with the subject I need your help with a financial transaction. SpamAssassin would rewrite the subject to become **Spam** (Had 12 hits, threshold is 5)-I need your help with a financial transaction.

If you choose not to have SpamAssassin rewrite the subject, you can still examine the headers of every e-mail that SpamAssassin scans because there will be a wealth of information there that you can use to see why SpamAssassin did or did not mark that message as spam.

The last five lines are for *whitelisted* addresses. These are addresses that SpamAssassin automatically marks as spam but that you feel should not be. Note that you can use * as a general wild card, or ? as a single-character wildcard. For example, *@sudom1234.org would permit any mail from the domain sudom1234.org to pass without being labeled as spam, ???@sudom1234.org would permit art@sudom1234.org through automatically, regardless of how many *hits* SpamAssassin finds in the message, while cart@sudom1234.org would be checked and labeled by SpamAssassin normally.

If you would like to learn more about SpamAssassin, you should consult the Packt title, *SpamAssassin: A Practical Guide to Integration and Configuration* [ISBN 1-904811-12-4] (http://packtpub.com/spamassassin/book).

SpamBox

SpamBox is a server-side method used to automatically filter out messages marked as spam by SpamAssassin. Note that the messages are not deleted. If you turn on SpamBox, the mail server will automatically place all spam into a special directory on the server. You can view it if you use the Horde or SquirrelMail web mail clients. You can also view it by appending /spam to the end of your e-mail account username in your e-mail client. When you do that, SpamBox will retrieve only the mail that it finds in the special spam directory on your server.

Spam Message Filter Configuration

Current Status

SpamAssassin is currently: enabled

Spam Box is currently: enabled

SpamAssassin

SpamAssassin is an automated mail filter that uses a wide range of heuristic algorithms on email headers and message bodies to identify "SPAM" (unsolicited email). SpamAssassin is designed to identify and mark emails that score beyond your threshold value. An email's SpamAssassin score is the sum of values given to certain known spam characteristics.

For more information, please visit the developers' website: http://www.spamassassin.org

To simply have the server DELETE and NOT deliver emails that are tagged as spam by SpamAssassin, click here now.

(Enable SpamAssassin)

(Disable SpamAssassin)

(Configure SpamAssassin (required to rewrite subjects))

Spam Box

This feature allows emails identified as spam by SpamAssassin to be delivered to a seperate mail folder named "spam". If this folder is not regularly checked and emptied, it may cause your email or filesystem quotas to be exceeded, resulting in a failure to receive legitimate messages. You can easily use IMAP or Horde/IMP to check messages that are routed to this box. If you wish to use pop3 to check the spam box, just add "/spam" (without the quotes) to the end of your pop3 login. (Example: user@domain.tld/spam)

This feature's use is generally discouraged in favor of sorting and deleting spam messages using your mail client. Without Spam Box you can configure SpamAssassin to mark your email with an identifying subject (e.g. ***SPAM***), which can then be filtered out into an appropriate location.

(Enable Spam Box)

(Disable Spam Box)

(Clear Spam Box)

If you are going to use your e-mail client to check the SpamBox, you will probably want to set up another account (or at least a filter) in your e-mail client so that when the SpamBox gets checked, the messages don't get dumped into your inbox, but get placed into another folder so it is easy to tell the messages apart.

If SpamAssassin is incorrectly labeling files, return to your cPanel and edit the SpamAssassin settings.

E-mail Filtering

Getting spam or other unwanted mail, and want to try to block some of it? Set up a filter to block e-mail based on your criteria. You can block based on the To: header, or the From: header, the subject line, a single word or words in the body of the e-mail, or any other header line.

Just select the criteria you want to block (one criterion per filter) and then click Activate. cPanel will even offer you the ability to test your new filters by running a test e-mail through your newly created filters to see if they work.

You can tell cPanel to delete any mail marked as spam by SpamAssassin by choosing the header as **SpamAssassin Spam Header** that **Begins With** and then typing **Yes** in the text box. Clicking the text **Click Here** just above the buttons to turn on, turn off, and configure SpamAssassin on the cPanel SpamAssassin screen, will accomplish the same thing.

BoxTrapper

Enabling BoxTrapper for any real, cPanel-created e-mail address in your managed domain turns on an anti-spam challenge and response system for that address. Note that this doesn't work for e-mail forwarding addresses (aliases). A similar feature is offered by several third-party companies, and some cost as much as much as 200 USD a year.

```
┌─ BoxTrapper Configuration ──────────────────────────────────────────────┐
│                                                                          │
│              Configure BoxTrapper for admin@domain.com                   │
│                                                                          │
│                  Current Status: enabled  (Disable)                      │
│                                                                          │
│                                                                          │
│   Configure     Edit Confirmation    Edit Forward/White/Black/Ignore  Review   Review │
│   Settings         Messages                    Lists                    Log     Queue  │
│                                                                          │
└──────────────────────────────────────────────────────────────────────────┘
```

If BoxTrapper is on, then any time an e-mail is received, it is placed into a special queue and BoxTrapper examines its whitelists for currently permitted e-mail senders. If the sender's e-mail address (or the e-mail subject line) is on the whitelist, the message is delivered immediately to your inbox. If the sender (or subject) is on the BoxTrapper blacklist, he or she gets an e-mail (which you can edit) notifying the sender that you are refusing mail from them.

If the sender (or subject) is on the BoxTrapper ignore list, then the e-mail is *not* delivered to your mailbox, and the sender is *not* sent a warning. If the sender and subject do not appear on any BoxTrapper list, they are automatically sent a *please verify* e-mail message which the user must respond to. Meanwhile, the message remains in the BoxTrapper queue awaiting a response. If one does not come, the e-mail is eventually deleted from the queue (in a user-specified number of days) and never delivered to your inbox. If the user responds, the user is placed on the BoxTrapper whitelist automatically and that message and all future e-mail from that sender will be immediately delivered to your mailbox. You can view the messages in the queue at any time and can set each message as good or bad or just delete them.

The operation is fairly straightforward. Enable BoxTrapper for any e-mail addresses you want to, then click Configure Settings to set how many different recipient e-mail addresses (perhaps through some forwarding or mailing list) get delivered to this address. If you have more than one e-mail recipient (perhaps support@domain.com and sales@domain.com both come to admin@domain.com, which is a real e-mail address, using e-mail forwarding for support@domain.com and sales@domain.com) then list them (admin@domain.com, support@domain.com, sales@domain.com) on the E-mail addresses going to this account line. Change the queue length if you want. If you get a lot of e-mail, you may wish to shorten the queue or you may run out of disk space. Next, edit the various confirmation e-mail addresses that BoxTrapper sends by clicking on Edit Confirmation Messages. Next, edit your blacklist/whitelist/ignorelist as you see fit. You can also review your current and past queues as well as see the log of what BoxTrapper received and what it did with those messages.

Virus Scanning using ClamAV

This feature isn't primarily designed to stop spam, though it can filter out some special kinds of spam (called phishing e-mail) that attempt to collect personal information about you by pretending to be an e-mail from your bank, PayPal, eBay, and so on.

```
Scanning for Virii

  Scanning:
  ... scan complete 30 files scanned.


  File:    1 / 30    Data:    0 / 0    M

                                              100 %


  Infected Files:
```

In addition, not all web hosts will offer this feature (or may offer something similar, but not exactly the same). If you host does offer it, you will find a link to Virus Scan on the main cPanel screen. Here you will be able to manually scan mail and the files in your account for viruses using a very good free virus-scanning engine called ClamAV. You can find out more information about ClamAV at its website, `http://clamav.net/`.

Default (Catch All) E-mail Address

Selecting Default Address will allow you to set what action the mail server will take when mail is sent to an e-mail address you have not set up a real e-mail account or e-mail forwarding for.

By default, cPanel is usually set to forward all mail to the default e-mail address (though your web host can change this default). Alternatively, you can set e-mail to non-existent addresses to be instantly discarded with no warning (set the action to :blackhole:) or have the e-mail bounced back to the sender with a message noting that the e-mail was undeliverable (set the action to :fail: no such address here). As a general rule, it is a good idea to leave the default e-mail address set to :fail:.

> You can put any words you like after :fail: and cPanel will use those words as the bounce error message. For example, :fail: Go away spammer! will send a bounce message telling the user to Go away spammer! Setting :fail: with no words after it will send a bounce message with no custom error message in the body.

E-mail Auto-Responders

Choosing Auto-responders from the cPanel mail manager screen allows you to have cPanel automatically send an e-mail response to anyone who sends a message to a particular e-mail address.

Modify/Add Auto-responder

Hint: If you do not create a forwarder or email account with the same address as this auto responder, mail sent to this autoresponder will only be handled by the autoresponder before it is discarded.

When configuring an autoresponder you can use the following tags to insert information into the message that is returned to the user:

%subject% The subject of the message that was sent to the autoresponder.

%from%   The sender of the message that was sent to the autoresponder.

%email%   The sender's email from the message that was sent to the autoresponder.

Email: presales   @ domain.com

From:

Subject   Re: %subject%

Character Set: us-ascii

HTML Message: ☐

Body:

Thank you for your interest in Wascally
Widgets, the world's premier widgets.

Current Pricelist:
Wowsers Widget US$10.00
Water Widget US$25.00
Willow Widget US$35.00
Walla-Walla Widget US$99.00

We accept Visa, Discover, Mastercard, American
Express and Paypal for payments.

If you would like to purchase a Wascally
Widget, please visit our website at:

http://domain.com/

Regards,

The Wascally Widget Team

(Create/Modify) (Clear)

This can be used for several different things. Perhaps the most common use is setting up an *on vacation* or *out of the office* message that automatically gets sent back to anyone who sends you e-mail. Be careful with this because if you subscribe to a mailing list, the mailing list could receive notification that you are away!

Another use might be to provide an e-mail FAQ covering commonly asked questions about a product or service you are selling, or about your company. So for example, you can create an auto-responder that automatically sends e-mail to a person who sends mail to techsupport@domain.com giving them answers to common problems and asking them to send mail to a different e-mail address if they still need help. If you specify a From address, then that auto-response message will only be sent to e-mail with that particular From address rather than to all messages received at that account. In addition, you can select the type of character set you want to use (for the language the e-mail message is written in) and even send out HTML mail this way, just click the HTML checkbox and type or paste in some HTML code. cPanel makes an attempt to keep track of which e-mail addresses it has recently auto-responded to in an attempt to stop infinite *I'm responding to your auto-response of my auto-response* messages. However, this system isn't perfect and doesn't always work, so you should be careful when using it.

Advanced E-mail Tools

These are a couple of features only used under special circumstances:

- **Change Primary E-mail MX Record**: You shouldn't change this unless you know what you are doing, as having it improperly set may cause all e-mail services to fail completely for your domain. This feature allows you to change the server that handles all incoming mail for this domain. Unfortunately, this cannot be used to add additional MX records (for backup mail service, for example). If you need extra MX records added to your domain, contact your web host.

- **E-mail Trace Tool**: This tool displays a map showing the mail server to which the e-mail is delivered. It will also help you to diagnose problems in sending mail to that address. It will map out any connections the address has and can provide information that may help tech support diagnose e-mail problems. It will be most useful for e-mail addresses not on the same server that you are on, since you will only see one entry for e-mail addresses on your server (as the mail doesn't get routed anywhere else).

Summary

In this chapter, you have learned:

- Why you may want to manage your own e-mail accounts
- How to setup and manage POP3 and IMAP e-mail accounts
- How to create e-mail forwarders and forward all e-mails from one account to another
- Ways to combat spam and viruses using features available in cPanel
- How to work with web mail
- How to manage mailing lists
- The more advanced features cPanel provides for working with e-mail

Hopefully you now feel comfortable enough with cPanel's e-mail features to try your hand at managing your own e-mail accounts.

In the next chapter you will learn how to work with databases using the tools available in cPanel. If you plan to use web scripts on your website or if you need some place to store data that can be sorted and displayed dynamically, you won't want to miss it.

5
Working with Databases

If you plan to do any work involving web scripts on your website, or if you need to store data on your website in a way that allows for dynamic retrieval of that data later, you will want to work with databases. cPanel includes a number of tools to make working with databases easier. In this chapter, you will learn how to:

- Create a database
- Create database users
- Add users to the database
- Change common connection settings for databases
- Delete databases and users
- Check for damage, repair, and optimize databases
- Work with databases using phpMyAdmin or phpPgAdmin
- Back up databases with phpMyAdmin or phpPgAdmin

Before you can learn how to use databases, however, we first need to figure out what they are and why we might need to use them.

Database 101

Defined generally, a **database** is a collection of information designed to make later retrieval easier. If you have ever used Microsoft Access or FileMaker Pro, you are probably familiar with databases. If not, then your eyes are probably beginning to glaze over. Databases aren't the most exciting tools you will use with your web hosting account, but they are arguably some of the most important.

cPanel supports two different types of databases at this time, MySQL and PostgreSQL. They both perform the same tasks, but they go about it in different ways. If your hosting plan comes with any databases, you will have access to MySQL. Whether or not you have access to both types of databases depends on your web host.

> cPanel currently has a more robust support for MySQL databases as compared to PostgreSQL databases.

The reason that having access to at least one database is important is that many web applications (scripts) require the use of a database to store information. Unless you plan to create a very simple website, you should make sure your hosting plan includes at least one MySQL database. Although it is possible for most scripts to all use the same database, you will find that it is easier and safer if you can create a new database for each script that requires one.

Working with Databases in cPanel

Clicking on the MySQL or PostgreSQL icons on the main cPanel screen will allow you to create or work with those types of databases. The interfaces that cPanel uses for both types of databases are remarkably similar and since most hosts only offer MySQL, we will focus on that (noting where the PostgreSQL interface differs from the one for MySQL).

```
Postgres Account Maintenance

                    Databases:
                domain_test  Delete

                Users in domain_test
                domain_test  Delete

    User: [domain_test ▲▼] Db: [domain_test ▲▼] (Add User to Db)

          Db: [                    ] (Add Db)

                      Users:
                domain_test  Delete
        UserName: [                    ]
        Password: [                    ]
                    (Add User)

                    phpPgAdmin
    You can use phpPgAdmin to administrate your Postgres databases in a
                    web based environment.
```

There are four main sections to the MySQL/PostgreSQL cPanel screen (referred to as the **database screen** from now on). The first section allows you to create and work with the databases themselves. The section below that allows you to create users that will be able to access one or more databases. Next, if your web host permits, you can set up remote access to your databases. Finally, there is a link to phpMyAdmin or phpPgAdmin, web interfaces for advanced work with your databases.

Creating a Database

Creating databases and users is easy but not the most intuitive process. The first thing you need to do to create a database is actually the last item in the database section. Type the name of the database into the Db: field and then click on the Add Db button. A database will be created and its name will be displayed at the top of the page.

> The actual name of the database will be slightly different from the one you choose. The database will be created with your cPanel username and an underscore character added to the beginning of the name you chose when you created the database, for example, domain_mydatabase.

Creating a Database User

Creating a database just creates an empty shell, waiting for data. Before you can use the database, you will need to put at least one user into the database. To create a new user, you need to type a username and password into the user section of the database screen and then click Add User. This will create a user with the password you define. Never leave the password field blank.

> The database username will be your cPanel username followed by an underscore and then the username you chose. For example, domain_jeff

Adding a User to a Database

You aren't done yet. You now have to associate at least one user with a database. Just above the Add Db field is a set of drop-down lists. The first of these allows you to select a user that you have already created and the second allows you to select the database that you want to associate with that user. Click Add User to Db and you are done. You can add a single user to multiple databases if you want to.

Once you add a user to the database you've created, you will notice that the listing for that database gets more detailed. It will show you the database name followed by some links to delete or repair the database and then it will show you every user in that database, along with sample code that shows you how to connect to the database in a PHP, Perl, or JDBC script (JDBC is only listed if your web host offers Java support).

Removing or Repairing a Database

Next to the username is a button marked Delete, but this can be deceiving because deleting a user from a database only removes the user from that database (and any records the user had in that database); it doesn't affect the actual user you created, which can still be active in other databases. Also, there is a Check button that allows you to check that database for problems, and then click Repair if it reports errors. If that doesn't do the trick, contact your web host for support.

phpMyAdmin and phpPgAdmin

At the very bottom of the screen is a link to phpMyAdmin (MySQL) or phpPgAdmin (PostgreSQL) that will open a new window with the phpMyAdmin or phpPgAdmin interface. These tools allow you to add, change, remove, backup or restore data in the databases you've created. Both tools are somewhat complex. It is beyond the scope of this guide to go into a lot of detail here about these very advanced tools. For example, we're not going to discuss database structure, or adding custom data. However, it is important to understand how to do at least a few basic things, since you may need to use it at some point.

> You cannot create new databases with phpMyAdmin or phpPgAdmin. You must use cPanel's MySQL or PostgreSQL interface to do that first and then you can work with the database in phpMyAdmin or phpPgAdmin.

phpMyAdmin

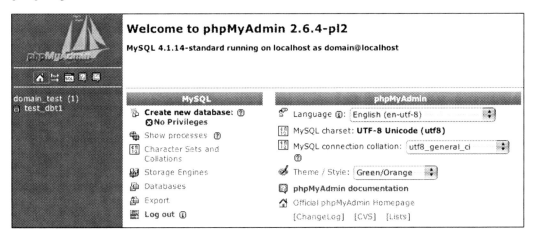

The main interface screen is divided into two sections, the database sidebar on the left and the main interface section on the right. On the right, you can set some basic interface and database preferences. You will also find a link to phpMyAdmin documentation that will explain each feature and option in some detail. On the left in the sidebar, you can select a database or table to work with by clicking its name.

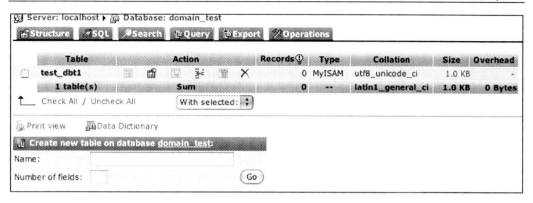

Once you select a database from the sidebar on the left, all of the main database categories will be listed. Clicking on a category shows you all of the data entries (rows) in that category on the main part of the screen. You can then add, delete, edit, or view any data in any row that you want. It is always advisable to make sure you have a current backup of any database you edit in case anything goes wrong.

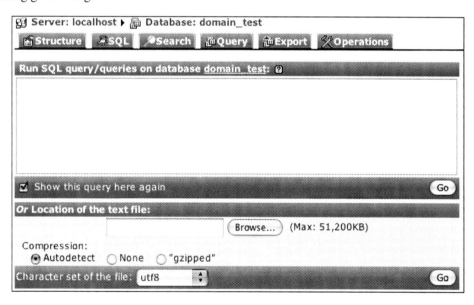

If you click the SQL tab along the top of the screen, you will be taken to a screen where you will be able to enter MySQL commands. Look for the large text entry box. This is where you can type in (or paste in) MySQL commands (which are commonly called queries). You can also paste in SQL file data (which you create using the export feature in phpMyAdmin) here to restore or add to the currently selected database. You can also specify the local file to use instead of pasting in data manually. This file must be a valid MySQL SQL file and can optionally be compressed. Click the Go button to submit the command/query and MySQL will tell you the results of the command (success or failure due to an error).

If you are pasting in many SQL commands or restoring a large SQL file (perhaps to restore a large database), you may have problems with phpMyAdmin *timing out* (stopping work) before the SQL has been executed. If so, you should try copying and pasting in smaller chunks of code, one at a time in order.

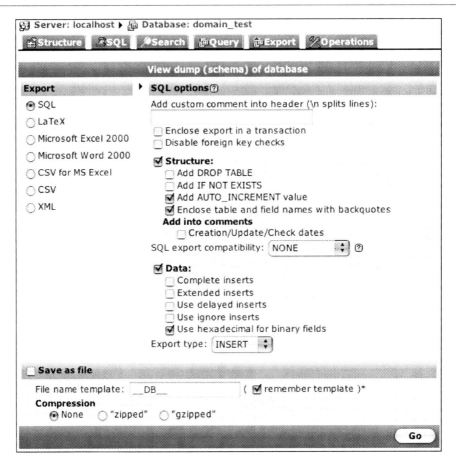

Clicking on the Export tab will allow you to export the data in the currently selected database in numerous different ways. You can use the export feature to back up databases. Typically, you will want to export an SQL file (which is a plain text file with SQL statements and can be restored using the SQL screen). The default SQL options are usually acceptable for backup purposes. To save this backup as a file, check the Save as File checkbox near the bottom of the screen. The file will be given a name based on the template listed. The default is usually acceptable. Choose to compress the file if your web host supports it, since the resulting file is much smaller. Click Go to export the database with your settings.

If you have problems exporting a database using phpMyAdmin, you should try to use cPanel's database backup feature discussed in Chapter 8. If for some reason you still cannot back up your database, please contact your web host for assistance.

To learn more about phpMyAdmin, you can refer to the Packt Publishing title, *Mastering phpMyAdmin for Effective MySQL Management* [ISBN 1-904811-03-5] (http://packtpub.com/mastering_phpmyadmin/book).

phpPgAdmin

phpPgAdmin is similar to phpMyAdmin, except that it is designed to work with PostgreSQL databases.

The first time you access phpPgAdmin you will need to log in for each session. When you click the **phpPgMyAdmin** link, the login screen will come up with the username and password filled in (it should match your cPanel username and password). Click the button to log in and you will see a screen like this:

As with phpMyAdmin, the sidebar on the left contains the databases you have created in cPanel. The center pane contains links to information about PostgreSQL and phpPgAdmin, which you should consult for specifics on working with PostgreSQL databases and phpPgAdmin. The bar at the top contains basic information about PostgreSQL, your account, and some links to areas of phpPgAdmin.

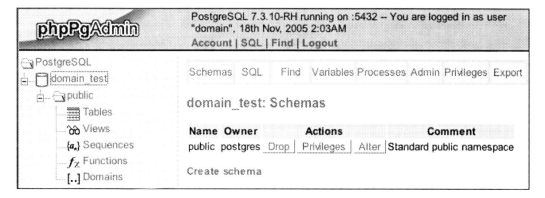

Clicking on a database in the sidebar takes you to a screen where you can manage that database. By default, you can modify database schemas (the information model) on this screen. Clicking on one of the links on the sidebar will allow you to focus on tables, views, and so on. Above the main content is a navigation bar that allows you to navigate to different features of phpPgAdmin (which work with the database you've selected in the sidebar at the left).

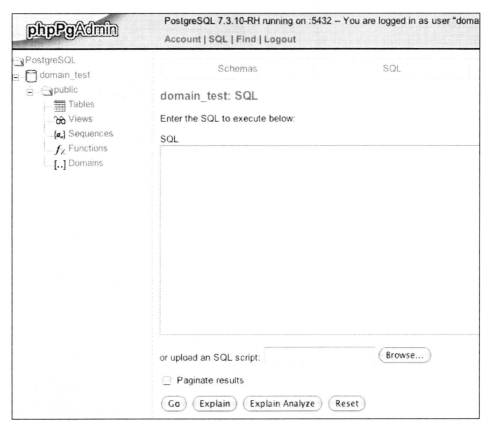

Clicking on the SQL tab allows you to input, find, or change data in the currently selected database. This is also the only way to restore PostgreSQL databases from a backup that you've made. Unlike MySQL, cPanel does not currently have a way to automate the backup and restoration of PostgreSQL databases. You need to use the export feature and then import the data via SQL data copied and pasted into this screen or via an SQL file saved on your local computer. If you have problems executing large numbers of SQL statements, contact your web host for assistance.

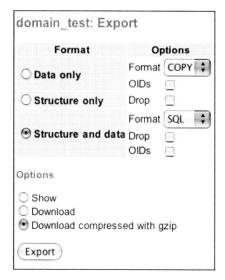

Clicking the Export tab allows you to back up the currently selected database to a file, or have the raw code displayed on screen. If you want to save the file for a backup later, you should select the Structure and Data SQL format and download the file with or without compression.

Downloading the compressed database will make the download much smaller. However, your web host needs to support server-side **gzip** compression for this to work. If you try to download the compressed file, and have problems, try downloading the uncompressed version.

Summary

In this chapter, you learned how to create, edit, and delete databases and database users using the tools available in cPanel. You also learned how to use phpMyAdmin or phpPgAdmin to perform common tasks with databases including backing up and restoring data.

In the next chapter, we will explore the many features that cPanel offers to organize and protect the content on your website.

6
Controlling Access to and Organizing Your Data

While you've probably purchased your web hosting account to share at least some information with the public, that doesn't mean you want all of the data on your site accessible by everyone who happens to stumble on it. In some cases, you may want to organize your data to make it easier to find and, at other times, you might want to restrict data access to yourself or to a select few trusted individuals. cPanel has numerous features that make such control simple. In this chapter, you will learn how to:

- Change your main cPanel password
- Create and manage subdomains
- Use redirects to send visitors and search engines to other web pages
- Enable hotlink protection and use it
- Manage leech protection
- Password-protect directories
- Stop users from visiting your site with the IP deny manager
- Create custom error messages

We'll start by looking at one of the most important features that cPanel offers to help keep your data secure.

Changing your cPanel Password

Regularly changing your password to a random, long, hard-to-guess one is a critical cornerstone in keeping your web hosting account safe from those who would seek to destroy your site or steal sensitive content. It is recommended that you change your password once a month.

Password Maintenance

This changes the main password for your account; please make sure you close all existing windows that you have open for the control panel.

Please do not make your password too simple and always write it down in a safe place.

Old Password:

New Password:

New Password (again):

(Change your password now!)

Protect your password:

Don't write down your password, memorize it. In particular, don't write it down and leave it anywhere, and don't place it in an unencrypted file! Use unrelated passwords for systems controlled by different organizations. Don't give or share your password, in particular to someone claiming to be from computer support or a vendor unless you are sure they are who they say they are. Don't let anyone watch you enter your password. Don't enter your password on a computer you don't trust. Use the password for a limited time and change it periodically.

Choose a hard-to-guess password:

Our system will try to prevent you from choosing a really bad password, but it isn't foolproof; create your password wisely. Don't use something you'd find in a dictionary (in any language or jargon). Don't use a name (including that of a spouse, parent, child, pet, fantasy character, famous person, or location) or any variation of your personal or account name. Don't use accessible information about you or your environment, such as your phone number, license plate or social security number. Don't use a birthday or a simple pattern, such as backwards, followed by a digit, or proceeded by a digit. Instead, use a mixture of upper and lower case letters, as well as digits or punctuation. When choosing a new password, make sure it's unrelated to any previous password. Use long passwords (say 8 characters long). You might use a word pair with punctuation inserted, a pass phrase (an understandable sequence of words), or the first letter of each word in a pass phrase.

After logging into your cPanel account, you can change your password by clicking Change Password. This changes your administrator password, which is used to log in to your cPanel mail, FTP, and SSH accounts. Keep in mind that if you change your password, you will need to follow cPanel's rules for a *safe* password:

- The length of the password should be greater than 6 characters
- It should not include any words found in a dictionary
- It should contain at least one number
- It should contain one or more non-alphanumeric characters

It is strongly recommended that you also take the advice cPanel provides about protecting your password.

Your web host may also permit you to automatically change your cPanel password if you have forgotten it. To do this, you must have a valid e-mail address entered into the cPanel contact e-mail address area (see Chapter 1) *before* trying to change your password.

To start the process of having your cPanel password reset, you must attempt to log into cPanel and then click cancel when you are asked for your username and password. You will be taken to a page where you can try logging in again. However, just below the login box, you will have a place to enter your cPanel username if you've forgotten your password and want to reset it. After entering your username and clicking the Click Here button, cPanel will send a special confirmation e-mail to the e-mail address you have specified in cPanel's e-mail contact information section. When you receive that e-mail, you will need to click on a special link or manually cut and paste the special link into your browser. Accessing that link will cause cPanel to generate and display a new password for your account, which takes effect immediately. Log in again using your cPanel username and new password. If for some reason, this does not work or you do not have the option to reset your password, please contact your web host for assistance.

Subdomains

Subdomains are addresses like subdomain.domain.com. The subdomain can either act as if it were an entirely different site, not part of your primary domain (using the *Add-on Domains* feature discussed in Chapter 10) or it can serve as a *shortcut* to redirect you to another place either in your site or to anywhere on the Internet.

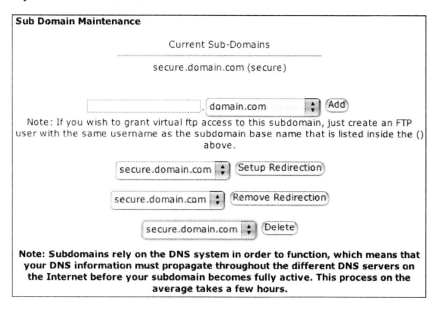

To create a subdomain, just type the subdomain you want into the field next to your domain name, then select the domain name you want the subdomain to be a part of and click Add. It is interesting to note that you can select subdomains that you have already created from this list. Therefore, it is possible that if you created a subdomain my at domain.com, you could subsequently create a subdomain is at my.domain.com ending up with is.my.domain.com and then finally adding this to come up with this.is.my.domain.com.

All subdomains default to loading the index page in a similarly named directory. For example, if you create the subdomain, gallery.domain.com, it will attempt to load pages found inside the directory gallery found inside your public_html directory. Don't try to add a redirect to the same directory that the subdomain points to by default or you will get a maximum redirection error (or just a blank white page depending on your browser) when you try to visit the subdomain since it now points to the same directory infinitely.

Keep in mind that it may take several hours before everyone on the Internet can access your new subdomain since the **DNS** (Domain Name Service) records need to be updated. In practice, however, most people should be able to access it almost immediately, but if not, don't panic.

If you want the subdomain to redirect to a different location, all you have to do is to select it from the Setup Redirection drop-down list in the Subdomain Maintenance area and then click the button next to the list of subdomains. This will take you to another screen where you can type in the exact address (including the http:// or ftp://) that you want the subdomain to point to and click Save. If you decide later that you want to remove this subdomain redirection, select the subdomain out of the drop-down list next to the Remove Redirection button and then click that button. To delete the subdomain altogether, just select it from the delete drop-down list and click the Delete button.

What if you want the subdomain to have its own web directory (perhaps you have a family member or user who wants their own web space)? You need to create the subdomain and then go to the FTP Manager in cPanel and create a new FTP account that has exactly the same name as the subdomain you created (without the primary domain name). For example, if you create a subdomain webmasters.domain.com then the FTP account you create should be called webmasters. This will create a directory in your public_html directory called webmasters. If you put an index.htm file in this directory, then that page will automatically get displayed when someone types in http://webmasters.domain.com/. In addition, that person's website could also be accessed by going to http://domain.com/webmasters/. They would connect to that subdomain directory via FTP using the username wemasters@domain.com and the password assigned to that FTP account. They would only be able to access /public_html/webmasters or any directory found inside webmasters. They would not be able to access the public_html directory or any other directory, above or at the same level as webmasters.

Redirects

Redirects are designed to help you keep the flow of your website while redirecting users and search engines to the new location for content that has moved. Here you can specify a redirect in the form, `http://domain.com/redirectname` that will instantly take you to any web address you specify.

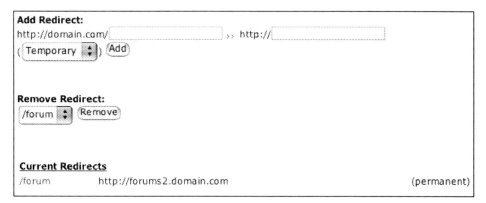

A temporary redirect is used for content that may have moved to a new location, but isn't going to be there forever. This sort of redirect generates a 302 (resource has moved temporarily). It doesn't much matter to end users, but this code tells search engines not to update the resource location with the new URL. A permanent redirect (which generates a 301 code) tells search engines that the new location is permanent and they should update their records and stop linking to the old URL for that resource.

Hotlink Protection: Stop People from Stealing Content

If you run a website where digital content (pictures, files, and so on) is your livelihood, then you may want to turn on this feature. Hotlink protection will stop people on other websites linking directly to your files unless they have approval from you.

Hotlink protection is currently enabled

HotLink protection prevents other websites from directly linking to files (as specified below) on your website. Other sites will still be able to link to any file type that you don't specify below (ie. html files). An example of hotlinking would be using a <img> tag to display an image from your site from somewhere else on the net. The end result is that the other site is stealing your bandwidth. You should ensure that all sites that you wish to allow direct links from are in the list below. This system attempts add all sites it knows you own to the list, however you may need to add others.

Enable Hotlink Protection:
Urls to Allow Access:

```
http://domain.com
http://secure.domain.com
http://www.domain.com
http://www.secure.domain.com
```

Extensions to allow (seperate by commas): `jpg,jpeg,gif,png,bmp`
Url to Redirect to:

☐ Allow direct requests (ie. entering the url to an image in your browser)

(Activate)

Disable HotLink Protection:

(Disable)

To turn this on you need to define:

- The list of domains that are permitted to link to your files. cPanel will automatically add any of your own domains to the list of approved domains but feel free to edit these as needed.

- The list of file extensions (JPG, MP3, and so on) that you want to protect. cPanel will automatically add a list of common file extensions but feel free to edit these as needed.

- A URL to redirect people to if they try to hotlink to your files (typically a page on your site that says Sorry, you can't access this file unless you are a member of my site.)

- If you want to allow people who manually type an address pointing to one of the files on your website to access the file or if you want them redirected to the same URL you entered above. To allow direct links, click the checkbox just above the Activate button.

Click Activate to turn on hotlink protection. Click Deactivate to stop using hotlink protection.

> Do not try to use this feature if you have FrontPage extensions installed (it won't work). If you use FrontPage extensions, you need to use Microsoft FrontPage itself to manage hotlink protection.

Password-Protect Directories

Do you have content in your website that you would like to restrict access to? cPanel makes the process fairly painless. The first thing you have to do is to create a directory inside your public_html directory that will contain your protected content. You can name it whatever you like. You can use your FTP client to create this directory or you can use cPanel's file manager described earlier. Now come back to the Password Protection area. You will see a list of every directory inside your public_html directory and a link for the *current folder* (which is your public_html directory in this case). If you click the small icon of a folder next to the directory's name, you will be able to see any directories nested inside that one. This way you can choose to protect a nested directory. If you click on the actual name of the directory, you will be taken to the security and account creation screen.

There are actually two separate things to do on this screen. The top half of this screen turns security on and off for this directory. If you want security to be on, then click the checkbox next to the Directory requires a password to access via the web item. Below that is where you can enter a short name or phrase that will appear in the dialog box that pops up asking you for your username and password. This item is purely optional, but it is a nice touch so that your users know what area they are trying to log into, in case there is more than one secured area. If you are done you can click Save and security will be set for that folder/directory.

You also need to create at least one authorized user or no one will be able to access the files in this directory unless they log in as the administrator via FTP. To create a username and password, just type them into the appropriate boxes and then click the Add New User button next to the Username field,. This user will now appear in the Active Users list, which means they now have access to this directory. Create as many users as you need. If you need to change the password of a user that has already been created, then just type the user's exact username and then type in a new password and then click the button next to the password field, Change Password. You will then be notified that the password for that user has been changed. When you are all done, then you can click Save to commit all the changes you made. If the directory has been successfully secured, you will see a small lock icon next to the folder icon for that directory. You cannot password-protect the public_html directory via this feature in cPanel.

Do not try to use this feature if you are using the FrontPage extensions. FrontPage handles page security through those server extensions rather than using the standard directory protection feature. If you have password protection set in cPanel and you install the FrontPage extensions, then all of your settings for password protection will be deleted and you will need to use FrontPage to manage security until you remove the FrontPage extensions, at which time you will have to re-enter all password protection information into cPanel.

Leech Protect: Keep Users from Giving Away Access to your Site

If you sell access to content on your website, some users may decide they will buy or create a single user account and give the account out to other people to use free. Leech protection helps stop this practice. At the time of writing, the Leech Protect feature is something that not all web hosts offer since it is not part of the core set of cPanel features.

Turning on Leech Protect watches your secured directories to see how often each user is accessing your protected directories. If the user goes over the maximum number of logins in any 2-hour period (you set the maximum number), Leech Protect will either e-mail you, or block the user's account, or both (as you choose).

This feature can be useful if you have a *members-only* section of your website controlled by cPanel's password-protected directories feature (which is really just a front end for Apache's standard password protection features). However, this cannot be used if you have Microsoft FrontPage extensions installed, as FrontPage uses a different and incompatible security model. You need to remove the FrontPage extensions and enable password-protected directories (at least one) before you can use Leech Protect properly.

Index Manager

Typically, if you try to access a directory (rather than a file) that exists on your server, and there isn't an *index* page (index.html, index.htm, index.php, default.html, default.htm, default.php) your web browser will display a list of all the files in that directory. You can then click on any of the files to view or download them. If you don't want to allow people to do this (a good idea if you have sensitive files stored in a directory inside your public_html directory), then you can use the Index Manager to turn off directory listing on a per-directory basis.

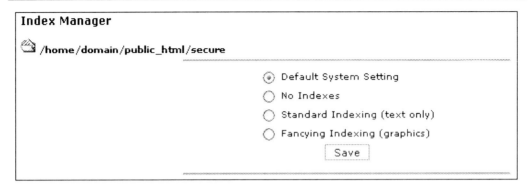

Just click on the directory you want to turn on/off directory listing in and then choose the level of protection you desire. Leave the directory set to the default system setting, do not allow any directory indexing, provide only a plain text listing of documents, or provide a list that includes text links and small graphics to represent the type of file or directory the item listed is. Click Save to commit your changes to that directory.

IP Deny Manager

If you find that people from a particular location are abusing your website (check your error logs and raw Apache logs), you can choose to block their IP address.

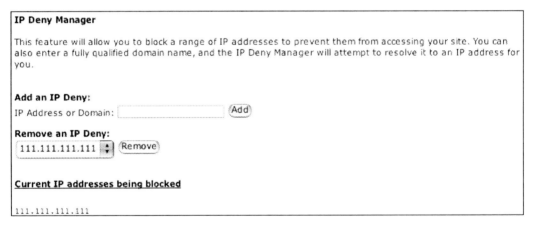

You can block a particular address from accessing your site, or you can block an entire range of IP addresses from being able to access your site. This area will also list any IP addresses that you are currently blocking. For example, 111.111.111.111 will block only that IP address, whereas entering 111.111.111 will block *all* addresses from 111.111.111.0 to 111.111.111.255, both inclusive. This will only block people from accessing your website and not other services such as mail, FTP, and so on.

Custom Web Error Messages

Let's face it, errors happen. It could be that a typo or missing page sends your users to a page that doesn't exist, or perhaps your server is having *issues*. In any case, you have the option of creating custom pages that your server will display when that error happens. Each custom page you can edit is referred to by the error number. What are these error numbers and what do they mean? Look at `http://htmlcenter.com/tutorials/tutorials.cfm/66/General/` to know more.

Probably the most common error is type **404**, which just means that the user has tried to access a page that doesn't exist on the server. If you've been using the Internet for more than a few days, you've probably seen this error before.

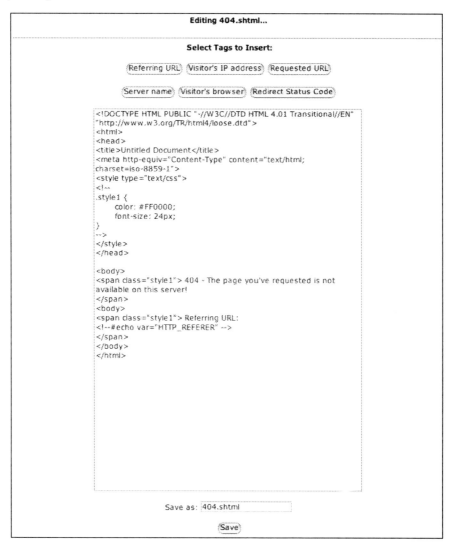

With cPanel, you can create custom pages to display a more friendly error message or to make that message match the style of your website. Just click on the number of the error that you want to create a custom error page for from the list in cPanel, then enter HTML code into the text entry area and click Save. You don't have to worry about editing the saved file name. If you want to add special tags to your error message to display the user's web browser, the page they were trying to access, and so on, you can click the appropriate tag button at the top of the text entry area. Clicking one of these buttons will insert a special line of code at the end of your current document. You can cut and paste this tag wherever you would like that information to appear in your error page.

Of course, error message editing in cPanel is provided as a quick-and-dirty way of getting the custom page you need created with a minimum of fuss. It doesn't display or render HTML code. If you aren't good at analyzing or editing raw HTML code, feel free to create your own custom error page in your favorite HTML editor (Adobe GoLive, Macromedia Dreamweaver or Contribute, and so on). Save the custom error page with the number of the error and append .shtml (for example 404.shtml) then save that file in your public_html directory on your server.

One thing to keep in mind is that by default some older versions of Internet Explorer for Windows display their own custom error pages unless the custom page on your server is larger than 10K in size, so your users may never see your finely crafted masterwork.

Summary

In this chapter, you learned how to control access to the data on your website in various ways. You now know how to change your cPanel password, how to use subdomains, redirects, hotlink protection, leech protection, the IP deny manager, and custom error messages to organize your data and make sure people only access the content that you want them to.

In the next chapter, you will learn how to monitor what people are doing on your website and what resources are being used.

7
Keeping an Eye on Account Activity

cPanel offers a number of features designed to allow you to keep track of what is happening in your account. We need to learn how to use these features to full advantage because visitors abusing your site can lead to it being suspended or worse. We will focus on:

- How to work with the various web statistics packages that cPanel offers
- How to disable and re-enable web statistics packages using the Stats Manager
- When and how to use your site's raw web logs
- How to keep track of the disk space your files are taking up
- How to use your cPanel error log to track down problems

The first stop on our tour concerns web statistics.

Web Statistics: What's Going On?

If your website is designed to attract public attention, (as opposed to a site that you only want friends and family to visit) then you need some way to keep track of who is visiting your site and what they are doing while they are there. Knowing what pages or files are most popular and who visits them can help you improve your website layout and even increase traffic to your site. However, it isn't practical to require every visitor to register or answer a poll or survey every time they stop by your site.

Raw (Apache) Web Logs

Thankfully that is not necessary in most cases, since most visitors automatically provide your site with basic information about where they came from, how they found your site and what sort of computer they are using during this visit. These data are called **web statistics**. The information is stored in a special file called a raw web log. A raw web log is essentially a text file with information about every person or machine that visited your site and what they requested in the order those requests were made. This file can grow to be quite large and very difficult to interpret. The average raw web log contains entries that look something like this:

111.111.111.111 - - [31/Oct/2005:12:22:57 -0500] "GET /gallery/download/1000/movie.zip HTTP/1.0" 200 105493 "http://domain.com/gallery/download/1000/" "Mozilla/4.0 (compatible; MSIE 5.0; Windows 98)"

In the above example, 111.111.111.111 is the IP address of the user that made this request followed by the date and time of the request. The request that was made of your website appears in quotes (in this case, the user is trying to get (download) a file called movie.zip from within the 1000 directory on your site). The **status code** is listed next (200). A status code lets you know what happened with this request. In this case, 200 tells us that the file was successfully downloaded.

> If you would like to know what a status code means, you can view the full list with explanations at http://w3.org/Protocols/rfc2616/rfc2616-sec10.html.

The size of the downloaded file is listed in bytes (1,024 bytes = 1 Kb). The exact URL request is listed next. Finally, some information about the user's web browser and computer platform is listed.

There will be one of these lines in the raw web log for every click (commonly referred to in web logs as a **hit**) a user makes while visiting your site. There may be hundreds or even thousands of hits for each visit a user makes to your website (often called a **session**).

You can download the raw web log for your website by clicking on Raw Access Log in cPanel. You will be presented with a list of the raw web logs for your account (including all parked domains, add-on domains, and subdomains). Click one to download it to your computer (the file will be compressed). You can also download your raw web logs via FTP by using one of the special FTP URLs provided at the bottom of the FTP Account screen (see Chapter 3 for more information about FTP and how to access these special links).

Either way, the raw web log will be compressed when you download it. You must uncompress it by using a program capable of handling *gZip* files like the free *Allume Stuffit Expander,* which can handle nearly any compression format and can be found at http://stuffit.com. The uncompressed log file will bear the same name as your website (domain.com). This name may cause some problems for you if you have a .com domain name when you try to open it since .com files are typically DOS command files (similar to an application on Windows or Mac OS X). You may want to rename the file to domain.txt so double clicking on it will open the file in a text editor.

Raw Log Control

You can control how raw logs are handled by cPanel by clicking on the Raw Log Manager from the main cPanel screen. Here you can tell cPanel to save old raw web logs to your home directory at the end of every month so you can access them later. cPanel typically removes raw web logs at the end of each month unless you say otherwise. You can also save every old month or only the most recent past month (if it is November now, cPanel saves only October's old raw web logs). Save changes when you have it set the way that you prefer. Below the Save button are links to download old compressed web logs for your main domain and any add-on domains or subdomains.

Web Stats to the Rescue!

As you can imagine, this can make the raw web log for even a modestly busy website nearly impossible to interpret without some help. Thankfully, cPanel comes with several tools that make interpreting all this data much easier. These tools are called **web stats programs**. They take the raw web log data and turn that data into manageable charts and graphs. The resulting data is much easier for mere mortals to understand.

To view the web statistics for your site, click on Web/FTP Stats in cPanel (there is a separate link for data only concerning subdomains called Subdomain Stats). From here you can access all of the tools cPanel provides to help you understand more about who is using your site and for what purpose.

Web / Ftp Statistics

In this area you can view statistics about your website. Please be aware that only latest visitors is a live feed. All of the statistical reports are updated every **12** hours. All of the bandwidth information is updated every **3** hours. If you wish to compare data from each statistics program you should only compare data that is at least **18** hours old to ensure that it has been updated and is providing the correct information. Please note these times are estimates, and are subject to change based on the amount of traffic on the server.

Analog
Analog produces a simple summary of all the people who have visited your site. It is fast and provides great lightweight statistics.

Awstats
Awstats produces very pretty stats.

Webalizer
Webalizer is a more complex stats program that produces a nice variety of charts and graphs about who has visited your site. This is probably the most popular stats engine available today.

Webalizer Ftp
Webalizer is a more complex stats program that produces a nice variety of charts and graphs about who has visited your site. This is probably the most popular stats engine available today.

Urchin Stats
Urchin is commercial stats package.

Subdomain Stats
This will show statistics for the subdomains on your account.

Latest Visitors
This will show you the last 300 visitors who came to your site and some interesting information about them.

Bandwidth
This will show how many bytes your account has transferred.

Error Log
This will show errors in your site, images not loading, missing files, etc. This is very useful for debugging CGI scripts.

---

cPanel automatically updates web stats information every 24 hours or however often your web host has set it to happen. Generating web stats takes a lot of server CPU time (often referred to as load). For this reason, most web hosts won't have the web stats set to update more than one time per day. If you need more up-to-date information use the update link at the top of the Awstats report (if your host offers it) or download your raw web log and use a web-log-processing program on your local computer to interpret the data. If you find that your web stats haven't been updated in a few days, contact your web host for assistance.

> Each web stats program may define exactly what constitutes a hit, session, or bandwidth use differently. This means that you will have some difficulty comparing the results between different web stats programs. You might want to find a program that you like best and only compare results from that one.

Analog

Analog doesn't use a lot of graphics to get its point across so you may prefer this if you are accessing cPanel with a dial-up connection as it will load the quickest.

Web Server Statistics for domain.com

Program started on Sun, Nov 20 2005 at 6:00 AM.
Analyzed requests from Tue, Jun 07 2005 at 5:30 AM to Sun, Nov 20 2005 at 5:59 AM (166.02 days).

General Summary

(**Go To**: Top | General Summary | Monthly Report | Daily Summary | Hourly Summary | Domain Report | Organization Report | Failed Referrer Report | Referring Site Report | Browser Report | Browser Summary | Operating System Report | Status Code Report | File Size Report | File Type Report | Directory Report | Request Report)

Figures in parentheses refer to the 7-day period ending Nov 20 2005 at 6:00 AM.

Successful requests: 3,986,097 (548,172)
Average successful requests per day: 24,009 (78,310)
Successful requests for pages: 275,156 (36,733)
Average successful requests for pages per day: 1,657 (5,247)
Failed requests: 182,339 (472)
Redirected requests: 2,351 (4)
Distinct files requested: 112 (16)
Distinct hosts served: 9,855 (1,281)
Data transferred: 3.12 terabytes (408.70 gigabytes)
Average data transferred per day: 19.22 gigabytes (58.39 gigabytes)

Monthly Report

(**Go To**: Top | General Summary | Monthly Report | Daily Summary | Hourly Summary | Domain Report | Organization Report | Failed Referrer Report | Referring Site Report | Browser Report | Browser Summary | Operating System Report | Status Code Report | File Size Report | File Type Report | Directory Report | Request Report)

Each unit (▪) represents 8,000 requests for pages or part thereof.

month	#reqs	#pages	
Jun 2005	1885	567	▪
Jul 2005	907	907	▪
Aug 2005	100	100	▪
Sep 2005	191	168	▪
Oct 2005	520913	31746	▬▬▬
Nov 2005	3462101	241668	▬▬▬▬▬▬▬▬▬

Busiest month: Nov 2005 (241,668 requests for pages).

Each section of the report that Analog produces has links to every other section so you can skip to the section you are interested in the most. Use your web browser's save page feature if you want to save the content of this particular report.

If you have any questions about how Analog works or how it defines terms like hits or sessions, or computes bandwidth, visit the Analog website at `http://analog.cx/docs/meaning.html`.

Awstats

Awstats uses more graphics than Analog, but it also provides more information about those visiting your website than Analog does.

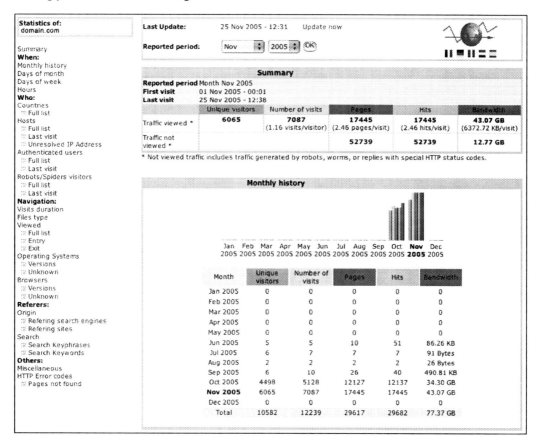

The Awstats report is divided into two sections, the sidebar with the name of your domain or subdomain that this report covers and links to the various sections of the report, and the main section. The top of the main section of the report contains links to any previous monthly reports and to update the report with up-to-the minute data (if your web host permits it). You can also click the picture of a flag to change the language the report is generated in.

> If your web host does permit the *update now* feature in Awstats be careful not to over-use it since it uses a lot of CPU load.

Below that are the various graphs and data of the report itself. Use the sidebar to scroll to the section you are interested in the most. To save this report you should use your web browser's save page feature.

Documentation on how to use Awstats and read the reports it generates can be found at http://awstats.sourceforge.net/docs/index.html.

Webalizer

Webalizer reports are graphic-rich and laid out on several pages. Webalizer provides about the same amount of information as Awstats does, but can also provide FTP-only reports that Awstats cannot.

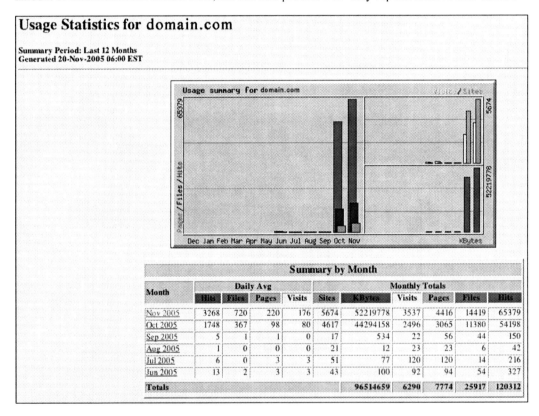

Usage Statistics for domain.com

Summary Period: Last 12 Months
Generated 20-Nov-2005 06:00 EST

Summary by Month

Month	Daily Avg				Monthly Totals					
	Hits	Files	Pages	Visits	Sites	KBytes	Visits	Pages	Files	Hits
Nov 2005	3268	720	220	176	5674	52219778	3537	4416	14419	65379
Oct 2005	1748	367	98	80	4617	44294158	2496	3065	11380	54198
Sep 2005	5	1	1	0	17	534	22	56	44	150
Aug 2005	1	0	0	0	21	12	23	23	6	42
Jul 2005	6	0	3	3	51	77	120	120	14	216
Jun 2005	13	2	3	3	43	100	92	94	54	327
Totals						96514659	6290	7774	25917	120312

The initial page of a Weblizer report provides monthly stats breakdowns. Clicking on the name of a month takes you to a separate page with in-depth information about the stats for that month alone. Saving this report is a bit trickier since it is spread across numerous pages.

Definitions of the terms that Webalizer uses can be found at the Webalizer website, http://mrunix.net/webalizer/webalizer_help.html.

Urchin

Urchin is a commercial web stats program that does not normally come with cPanel, but that your web host might offer. It provides extremely graphic-rich and detailed reports, but the reports are very large.

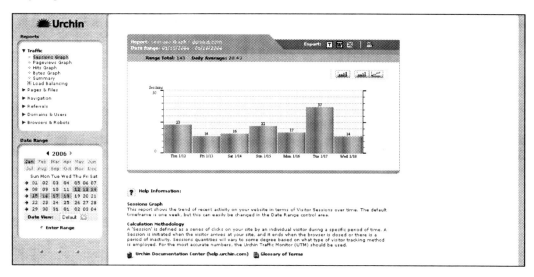

Urchin was recently purchased by Google and so support for the older versions of Urchin that cPanel supports is very limited. On a more positive note, Urchin online, now called Google Analytics, is free to use. You can find out more about Google Analytics at http://google.com/analytics/.

Statistics Configuration

This feature is found on the main cPanel screen if your web host offers it. Here you are able to turn on or off any web statistics packages that your web host offers. While having several different web stats programs might be nice, they do use disk space in your account. Some, like Webalizer and Urchin, can use vast amounts of disk space. I recommend that you try using each web stats program, find your favorite, and disable the others. Why waste disk space on web stats you do not use? If you don't use any of them, you can turn them all off.

Other Related Tools

While the web stats programs mentioned above offer a lot of data about visitors to your website, they are not the only tools that cPanel provides to help you figure out who is visiting your site and what they are doing while there.

Last Visitors

This tool parses the raw web log and displays the most recent visitors. The text explaining this feature in cPanel claims that it displays the last 300 visitors, but it actually displays the last 300 hits (clicks). This tool can take a few seconds to be displayed after you click on the Last Visitors link.

The display looks somewhat similar to the raw web log output, except that it is cleaned up and sorted by IP address of the visitor in reverse chronological order (most recent hits at the top). You can see which files or pages the visitor tried to access, when they visited, and some basic information about them.

Bandwidth

Each web stats program keeps track of bandwidth usage, but each stats program computes bandwidth differently. The bandwidth tool shows you exactly what bandwidth cPanel counts towards your monthly bandwidth limit, so you should use it to keep an eye on bandwidth rather than web stats programs.

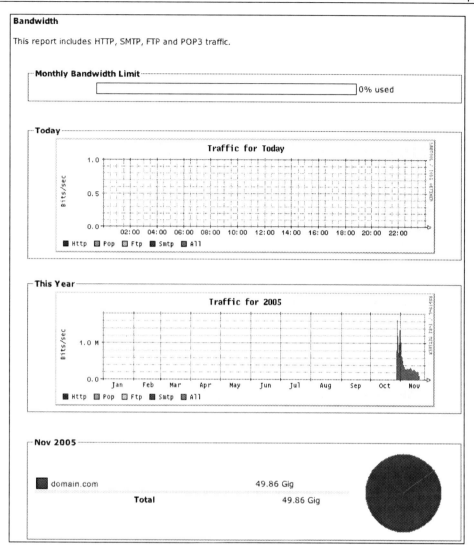

The bandwidth tool initially shows quick daily, monthly, and yearly bandwidth graphs. Clicking on the domain name or subdomain name in each month on the initial page will bring you to another page where you can view monthly bandwidth broken down by protocol (HTTP, FTP, and incoming and outgoing e-mail traffic). You can further break down bandwidth by each day of that month by clicking on the number of the day you wish to examine.

If you notice a serious discrepancy between the bandwidth the main cPanel screen shows and the amount that the bandwidth tool shows, please contact your web host to get this resolved.

Error Log

The error log shows you problems that people have had when accessing your website in the past few days. This can be very handy to help you figure out problems with pages on your website since any missing graphics or other such issues will be listed here. For example, if you try to access a page on your website and get error number 500 (Internal Server Error) more information about that error should be listed at the top of your error log.

Disk Usage

Disk usage is found as a separate item on the main cPanel screen. Clicking it will provide you with a breakdown of how much disk space is being taken up by every directory in your site. This is handy if you need to look for some files and directories to remove to free up some additional disk space. It is also useful if you allow people to upload items to your website, since you can keep track of how much space these uploads are using.

Disk Usage Viewer

Show Parent Directories | Show More Directory Depth
Show Less Directory Depth | Show Top Level | Clear File Usage Cache
Hide Small Files | Show File Sizes as bytes

Directory	Space Used
tmp/urchin	3.50 Meg
public_html/WysiwygPro	1.13 Meg
public_html/testgb	1.10 Meg
tmp/analog	0.11 Meg
public_html/cgi-bin	0.05 Meg
tmp/awstats	0.05 Meg
etc/domain.com	0.03 Meg
mail/admin	0.02 Meg
.neomail-admin/domain	0.02 Meg
.neomail/domain	0.02 Meg
tmp/webalizer	0.02 Meg
public_html/secure	0.02 Meg
.cpanel/nvdata	0.01 Meg
mail/domain.com	0.01 Meg
public_html/test	0.01 Meg
.htpasswds/secure	0.01 Meg
etc/secure.domain.com	0.00 Meg
public_ftp/incoming	0.00 Meg
public_html/entropybanner	0.00 Meg
tmp/webalizerftp	0.00 Meg
ssl/private	0.00 Meg
.fantasticodata/temporary	0.00 Meg
.fantasticodata/joomla	0.00 Meg
.fantasticodata/PerlDesk	0.00 Meg
mail/secure.domain.com	0.00 Meg
etc/.boxtrapper	0.00 Meg

The display starts with all top-level directories (the ones directly in your home public_html and public_ftp directories). Clicking the buttons at the top of the list changes what directories are displayed and can clear the file usage cache (which is typically updated about every 10 minutes). Clicking on a directory in the list will show only those items inside that directory and how much disk space they currently use.

Summary

In this chapter, you have learned how to use *web statistics* programs to keep track of how people are using your website. We also learned about some other tools that cPanel provides to help you keep track of things on your site.

In the next chapter, we will discover another important feature of cPanel, account data backup. Make sure you spend some time understanding Chapter 8, because having recent backups will save you from a wide variety of problems that might be catastrophic otherwise.

8

Backing up and Restoring Data

What can you do if you've deleted some critical data from your website or if you've had stuff deleted by someone or something else? How do you get all of that back quickly? cPanel's backup and restore features can help you get up and running again quickly. In this chapter, we will discuss:

- What backups are and why they are so important
- How to use cPanel to backup the data in your account
- What automated backup methods are
- How to use cPanel to restore the data that you've backed up
- What to do if you do not have a backup and need to restore the data in your account

Backups and their Importance

A **backup** is the copying of important data in case the original data becomes damaged or missing for some reason. Having a recent backup at all times of the data stored in your web hosting account is absolutely critical as it provides you a safety net if something untoward happens. Even if you web host's web server is 100% reliable and never has any problems (which is unlikely to be the case if you have a shared hosting account) there are still many ways in which data in your account could become corrupted or go missing:

- You could accidentally erase or overwrite important files
- Scripts you are using might be or become unstable and damage files
- Your website could be compromised by external forces (spammers, scammers, hackers, and so on), causing data to disappear or be altered

You may also need to refer to old data that you've removed.

Even if your web host tells you that they automatically back up the data in your account daily, it is still of the utmost importance that you plan personally to back up your account data regularly. Since, even if your web host will restore their backups of your data, they may not be able to do so quickly enough to save you from protracted downtime. Further, if your host has a problem with their backup of your site you will be out of luck.

Manually downloading all files in your account and using phpMyAdmin or phpPgAdmin to back up your databases (see Chapter 5 for more on working with databases and phpMyAdmin and phpPgAdmin) would make regular backups quite a painful process. Thankfully, you can download backups and even restore most files with just a few clicks from cPanel. To start the process, click on Backup in cPanel. You will be presented with a screen similar to the following:

Backup

Full Backups

Generate/Download a Full Backup
Note: You cannot restore these backups, they can only be restored by your administrator.

Home Directory

Download a home directory Backup

Restore a Home Directory Backup
[Browse...] [Upload]

Download a MySQL Database Backup

test

Restore a MySQL Database
[Browse...] [Upload]

Download Aliases or Filters Backup

Aliases   Filters
domain.com   domain.com
secure.domain.com secure.domain.com

Restore an Alias/Filter
[Browse...] [Upload]

The various backup options are listed on the left side of this screen. There are four main backup options:

- Full backup
- Home directory backup
- MySQL database backup
- E-mail aliases (forwarders) and filters backup

If you want to be able to restore your account files using cPanel's restore feature then you need to use the home, MySQL, and e-mail aliases and filters backup features.

> Backing up and restoring files via cPanel does not count against your monthly bandwidth limit, so feel free to do it as often as you need to.

Home Directory Backup

Clicking Download a Home Directory Backup will cause cPanel to compress all the files you see when you log into your account via the main FTP account (including the `public_ftp`, `public_html`, and `mail` directories). Depending on how many files you have in your home directory and how large they are this process can take anywhere from a few second to a minute or more. When the process is complete, you will be prompted to choose a location to save the compressed backup of your home directory on your local computer.

The filename of this backup will always be in the format `backup-domain.com-MM-DD-YYYY.tar.gz` where MM is two digits for the month, DD is two digits for the day, and YYYY is four digits for the year of the backup. This backup gets most of the files in your account, but it does not get mailman mailing lists, databases, or e-mail forwarders or filters (because these are stored outside of your home directory).

Database Backup

At the time of writing, cPanel only makes backups of MySQL databases. cPanel does not yet offer a feature to download or restore PostgreSQL backups yet. You will need to use phpPgAdmin's export feature to back up and restore PostgreSQL databases if you have any.

Every MySQL database that you have created will be listed in the MySQL Database Backup section. You will need to click on the name of each database to download them separately. cPanel will compress the database and allow you to download a copy to your local computer with the name `DBNAME.gz` where DBNAME is the name of the database (it should match the name of the link you clicked on to download the database backup).

E-mail Aliases (Forwarders) and Filters Backup

The table in this section will list your main domain, add-on or parked domain(s) and subdomains. If you've created any e-mail forwarders in cPanel (see Chapter 4) then you will want to click on each link under Aliases where you have created forwarders. The forwarders filename will be `aliases-domain.com.gz` where `domain.com` is the domain or subdomain name.

If you have created any e-mail filters (see Chapter 4), you should also click the links under Filters for each domain or subdomain for which you have created e-mail filters. The filters filename will be `filters-domain.com.gz`.

> Clicking on the aliases or filters link for a domain or subdomain that does not have any forwarders or filters set up will create a backup of a mostly empty file. cPanel's restore feature handles these files just fine, but why waste your time downloading empty files? However, if you are unsure if you've created forwarders or filters, download each file to be sure you get everything.

Full Backups

Full backups create a single, compressed file that contains everything from your account, including e-mail, mailman mailing lists, databases, and web content. Full backups, while easy to create and download cannot be restored from within cPanel. You have to manually restore files or ask your web host to restore the compressed full backup file for you.

Clicking on Generate/Download a Full Backup will take you to the following screen where you can edit a few settings and options related to full backups:

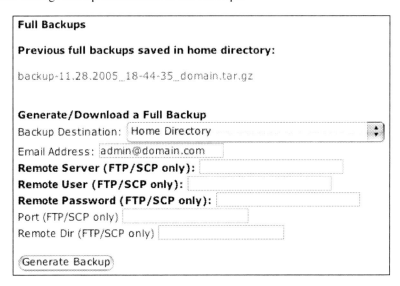

The drop-down box on this page allows you to set where the compressed full backup will be saved. You have a choice of saving it in your home directory (where you will be able to download it later) or a remote server via FTP (active or passive FTP) or SCP (Secure CoPy—similar to SFTP, more secure than FTP). If you want to have your backup sent to a remote server, you need to enter the information below the e-mail address. The remote server is the IP address or host name of the server. The user and password must be a valid user on the remote server. You can also change which port and directory the full backup is saved to, on the remote server. The e-mail address you enter will be sent a message when the backup is complete with the results of the backup (successful or not).

Click Generate Backup to begin the process of backing up your files (which can take anywhere from a few seconds to an hour to finish depending on how big your account is and how busy the server is). If you save your backup to your home directory, it will appear as a link at the top of this page. Clicking the link will start downloading the backup to your local computer. If the backup is not complete, the link will not be clickable and will note that the backup is still in progress.

Automated Unattended Backups

While backing up files with cPanel is very easy, remembering to log into your cPanel account regularly and create those backups may not be so easy. Thankfully, there are a couple of options if you want to automate the backup process.

- This script uses the standard cPanel backup feature to create a backup and then downloads the file and saves the backup. It requires a PC with DOS or Windows to run. http://absobblogginlutely.net/mtblogarchive/003217.php

- This third-party service promises to back up your entire cPanel account to one of its remote servers on a monthly, weekly, or daily basis for a fee. http://cpanelbackup.com/

Restoring Backups

If you have used the separate home directory, MySQL, and e-mail alias and filter backups (rather than the full backup feature), you can also restore these backups from the backup screen in cPanel. There are three separate places to restore the files you've backed up. All three are on the right side of the backup screen.

The first restore field is for home directory backups. Click Browse, select the compressed home directory backup file from your local computer, and click Upload to start the restore process. The file is first uploaded to your home directory and then it is decompressed and all the files restored. During the upload process, you won't see anything happening on your screen. Once the upload is complete and the home directory is being restored the screen will clear and you will see the progress updated regularly. Be patient, the entire process can take a long time if your home directory is large and if you have a dial-up connection to the Internet.

> Under no circumstances should you stop the restore process once it has begun restoring files, since doing so may render your account unusable. Wait until the process is complete and then click back in your web browser to get back to your cPanel and try the restore again if you need to.

The second restore field is for compressed MySQL database backup files. Like the home directory backup restore process, select one of the MySQL database files you wish to restore and click Upload. Wait until the restore is completed before clicking the back button in your web browser to restore another MySQL database.

The final field is to be used for both e-mail forwarder and filter backup files. Select one at a time and click Upload to restore it. Unless you have very complex filters or lots of forwarders set up this restore process should not take long. Click back when done to choose another filter or alias backup file to restore.

> If you have problems restoring the backups you have, please contact your web host for assistance.

Summary

In this chapter, you learned why regular backups of your account data are so important. You also learned how to use cPanel to back up, and restore files and send backups to remote servers via FTP or SCP.

In the next chapter, we will cover working with web scripts to enrich your website. Unless you prefer coding every aspect of your website personally, this is not a chapter you will want to miss.

9

Working with Scripts

You may be an expert at coding web pages and designing content or you may be a complete beginner. Regardless of your level of expertise, there will probably come a time when you want to add content or features to your website without spending days or weeks coding something or paying someone to create the content for you. This is where pre-coded web scripts may come in handy. In this chapter, we will cover:

- Scripts and what you might want to use them for
- Installing different scripts that cPanel offers
- Some important advice concerning working with scripts

Before we can take a closer look at the exciting world of web scripts, we first need to know what exactly these things are.

What are Web Scripts?

Web scripts are pages of code that are designed to be accessed on the Internet to accomplish a particular task. You can think of them like applications on the web. Each web script can be written in one of several different programming languages (PHP, Perl, Java, (D or X)HTML, and so on). There are hundreds of thousands of freely available web scripts that are designed to satisfy almost any need you might have without your having to personally create code from scratch. For example, perhaps you want to host photos on your website so others can view them or perhaps you aren't any good at working with HTML and would rather have some other program take care of the code so you can focus on the content. There are web scripts that can help you with both of these issues and many more. We will learn about several web scripts in this chapter.

Before you can use any web script, you need to know what programming languages your web host supports. To be sure, you will need to ask your web host. However, a few languages almost certainly supported are Perl (CGI), PHP, HTML (and XHTML and DHTML), JavaScript (do not confuse this with Java), and Python (CGI).

The Scripts cPanel Offers for Installation

Once you find a script you might want to use, you may find yourself with many questions: How do I install it on my site? How do I access its administrative features? How do I remove it if I decide later that it really isn't the best for my website? How do I go about upgrading it to a newer version?

You aren't alone. Many people have these same questions. Thankfully, cPanel comes to the rescue by allowing you to install, update, and remove many popular scripts with just a few clicks. In the following sections of this chapter, we will take a closer look at all of the many scripts cPanel has the ability to install by deafault.

The Scripts Library

Clicking on Scripts Library in cPanel will bring you to a screen that will allow you to access numerous scripts that cPanel can install, upgrade, or remove with just a few clicks. The exact number of scripts offered here will vary from one to nearly eighty (with the addition of some third-party add-ons). The ones mentioned below are those that cPanel itself offers by default. If you'd like more information about various third-party add-ons that offer additional script installation in cPanel, please see Chapter 12. The scripts in the Scripts Library are all written in PHP unless otherwise noted.

Every script in the Script Library is installed and managed in the same fashion. You click on the name of the script you are interested in and this takes you to a screen where you can manage installations of that particular script:

---

phpBB 2.0.18 Setup

> phpBB is a high powered, fully scalable, and highly customizable Open Source bulletin board package.

New Installation

Admin User: [   ]   Admin Pass: [   ]

Install at this url: http://domain.com/[   ] (Install)
(You must install in a top level directory. Example: 'http://domain.com/phpBB' is a valid place to install, but 'http://domain.com/user/andy/phpBB' is not.

Modify an existing Installation
testphpbb

Upgrade an existing Installation
[⬍] (Upgrade to 2.0.18)

Remove an existing Installation
[testphpbb ⬍] (Remove)

To install that script, fill in the few fields that may appear near the top of this screen (typically just an administrative username and password) then choose a subdirectory to install the script. The directory does not have to exist (cPanel will create it during the install process). If the directory you specify does exist, you should make sure that it is empty before trying to install the script. cPanel will refuse to install a script in a directory that already contains files. When you have finished entering the required information, click Install to install the script. cPanel will inform you if the installation was successful or not and provide the URL to access your new installation.

cPanel doesn't have the ability to install scripts directly in public_html. If you want people visiting your domain at domain.com, to go immediately to a particular script you have installed in a subdirectory, you can do so using an index.php file placed in public_html (make sure there isn't an index.html or index.htm file in this directory). The following code should appear in this index.php file:

```
<?
header ("Location: http://domain.com/scriptdir/");
?>
<html>
<title>Page Title</title>
<head></head>
<body>
</body>
</html>
```

Replace the URL after Location: in the code above with the URL to the directory where the script you want to use is installed. Also change the page title text between the HTML <title> </title> tags to whatever you want it to be.

Now when anyone accesses your domain, they will be taken immediately to the location where your script is installed.

Once you have installed a script, going back to the Script Library page for that script will also allow you to access the current installation(s) of that script via a link under Modify an Existing Installation.

You will also be able to upgrade any instances of that script that cPanel installed. To do so select the installed script under Upgrade an Existing Installation and click the Upgrade to Version Number button. cPanel will then upgrade the installation automatically and let you know the results. If there are no installations listed here, then all your installations are the latest version that cPanel can currently install.

> When you upgrade, you may lose any special customizations you added to the script (for example additional code or templates), so be careful.

You can have cPanel remove an installation by choosing the installation from the drop-down list under Remove an Existing Installation and clicking on Remove. cPanel will prompt you once to be sure you really want to remove the script and then do so and present the results on screen.

If you use cPanel to install a script you should always use cPanel to remove that script so that cPanel knows that the script has been removed. If you have manually removed a script, please inform your web host so they can remove the references to that script in cPanel's Script Library.

Advanced Guestbook

A guestbook is a script that allows people to write a short amount of text on a special page on your website. Typically, this is used to allow visitors to make short comments about your website or simply to say hello. Advanced Guestbook allows an administrative user to control posts and certain features of this script. It requires one MySQL database. For more information, refer to http://proxy2.de/scripts.php.

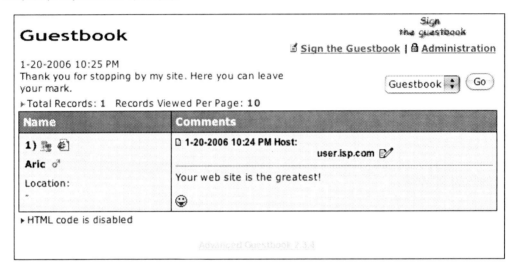

b2Evolution

b2Evolution is a **blog** script. Blog is short for web log. Blogs are a quick and easy method of creating and managing a website. Blogs are focused on content. It is very easy to add content to a blog. You don't need to know HTML or PHP to create a website. If you can type text, you can use a blog. Blogs are often used as web dairies that focus on whatever pops into the author's mind. b2Evolution requires a MySQL database. For more information, refer to http://b2evolution.net/.

Coppermine

Coppermine is a photo gallery script. Coppermine makes managing a large number of photos easy. It offers several themes and many features that make it quite popular. For more information, refer to http://coppermine-gallery.net/index.php.

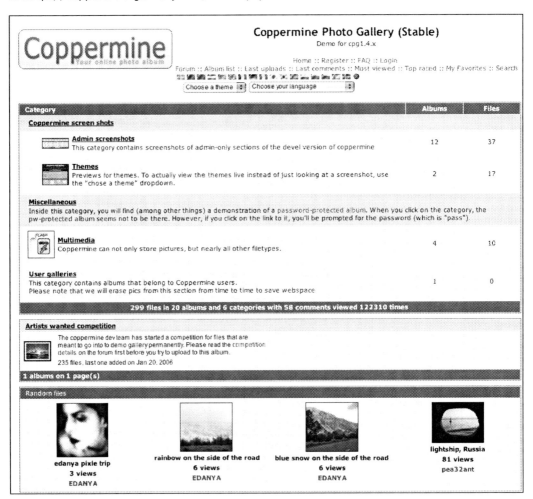

cPSupport

cPSupport is a CGI (Perl) helpdesk script created by cPanel Inc. It is currently in beta and so some features may not work as intended. It allows users to enter tickets via e-mail or an on-line interface, to which staff can then respond. These sorts of scripts come in handy if you are running a business where users might regularly come to you with questions. It requires a MySQL database. For more information, refer to `http://forums.cpanel.net/showthread.php?t=39751`.

e107

e107 is a Content Management System (**CMS**). CMS are designed to be flexible platforms for entire websites. A CMS takes care of the actual code of the website and allows you to focus on the content and basic layout. e107 requires a MySQL database. For more information, refer to `http://e107.org/news.php`.

There are many different CMS scripts and it can be hard to know which one might best fit your needs. Thankfully, at `http://opensourcecms.com/`, you can try out many of them before attempting to install one on your site.

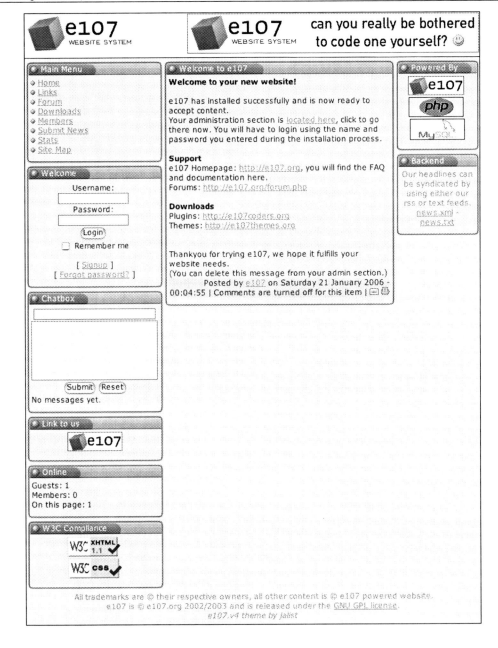

Geeklog

Geeklog is another blog script. It requires a MySQL database. For more information, refer to `http://geeklog.net/`.

Invision Power Board

Invision Power Board is a **forum** script. A forum is a meeting place where people interested in particular topics can post messages both publicly and privately. Invision Power Board (IPB) is now a commercial script without any free version. If your web host offers this, it is an older version that was a commercial script with an unlimited free trial. This forum script version is insecure and not being updated, so I do not recommend you use it. If you like the features it offers, you might want to consider paying for a copy of the current version (2.1 at the time of writing this book). For more information, refer to http://invisionpower.com/. You can also go through the Packt Publishing title *Invision Power Board 2: A User Guide* [ISBN 1-904811-38-8] (http://packtpub.com/invision_power_board/book).

Mambo Open Source

Mambo is a free CMS script. Mambo has quite a large following because it is flexible and easy to use. Recently the developers responsible for maintaining Mambo left the parent company (Miro) to start a new CMS based on Mambo. This new CMS, called Joomla! is very similar to Mambo and can even use most of the add-ons made for Mambo (http://joomla.org/). cPanel currently does not offer Joomla!. Mambo has a new set of developers now and continues as an active project. Politics aside, Mambo is a very capable script. It requires a MySQL database. For more information, refer to http://mamboserver.com/. You can also go through the Packt Publishing titles *Building Websites with Mambo* [ISBN 1-904811-73-6] (http://packtpub.com/mambo/book), *Mastering Mambo: E-Commerce, Templates, Module Development, SEO, Security, and Performance* [ISBN 1-904811-51-5] (http://packtpub.com/mastering_mambo/book), and *Building Websites with Joomla!* [ISBN 1-904811-94-9] (http://packtpub.com/joomla/book).

Nucleus

Nucleus is another CMS. It requires a MySQL database. For more information, refer to http://nucleuscms.org/.

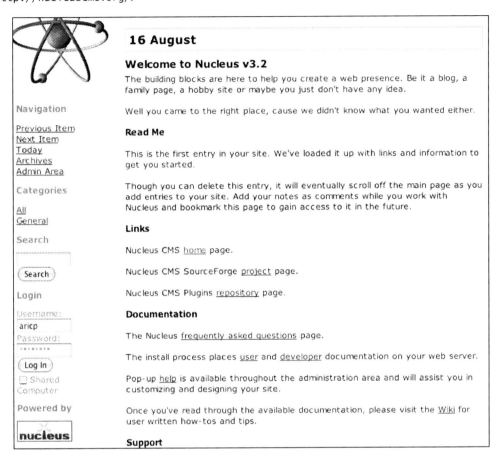

osCommerce

osCommerce is a popular and full-featured e-commerce (shopping cart) script. The problem with this script is that it can be a bit tricky to customize the look (which requires editing the code). In addition, development on this script moves very slowly. osCommerce has been at version 2.2 Milestone 2 for years now. This script requires a MySQL database. For more information, refer to `http://oscommerce.com/`. You can also go through the Packt Publishing titles *Building Online Stores with osCommerce: Beginner Edition* [ISBN 1-904811-88-4] (`http://packtpub.com/beginning_oscommerce/book`), or *Building Online Stores with osCommerce: Professional Edition* [ISBN 1-904811-14-0] (`http://packtpub.com/professional_oscommerce/book`).

PHP-Nuke

PHP-Nuke is one of the most popular CMS scripts in the world. It has many features and is quite easy to use, which makes it popular with those people not very familiar with how CMS scripts work. Unfortunately, it is very insecure. At the time of writing, every publicly released version of this script has serious flaws that make it easy for hackers to exploit. I recommend avoiding PHP-Nuke and choosing a more secure CMS. For more information, refer to http://phpnuke.org/. You can also go through the Packt Publishing title *Building Websites with PHP-Nuke* [ISBN 1-904811-05-1] (http://packtpub.com/phpnuke/book).

phpBB

phpBB is a very popular forum script. Recently, phpBB has been discovered to have a number of serious security flaws (all of which were fixed shortly after being disclosed) but hackers love trawlling for older versions of phpBB, so make sure you always keep phpBB up to date if you use it. phpBB requires a MySQL database. For more information, refer to `http://phpbb.com/`. You can also go through the Packt Publishing title *Building Online Communities with phpBB 2* [ISBN 1-904811-13-2] (`http://packtpub.com/phpBB/book`).

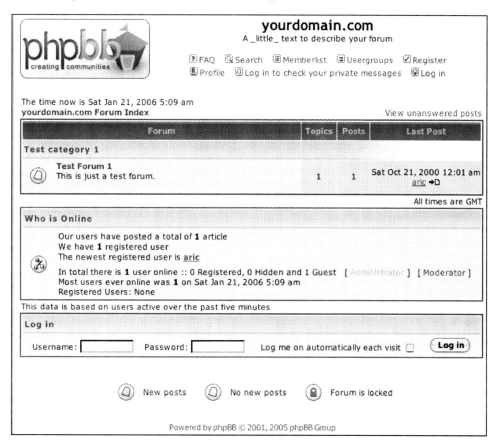

phpWiki

phpWiki is one of a number of popular **wiki** scripts. A wiki is online collaborative software somewhat similar to a blog, except anyone can add or edit information if permitted. phpWiki requires a MySQL database. More information: `http://phpwiki.sourceforge.net/`

---

php wiki # Front Page

- What is a <u>WikiWikiWeb</u>? A description of this application.
- Learn <u>HowToUseWiki</u> and learn about <u>AddingPages</u>.
- Use the <u>SandBox</u> page to experiment with Wiki pages.
- Please sign your name in <u>RecentVisitors</u>.
- See <u>RecentChanges</u> for the latest page additions and changes.
- Find out which pages are <u>MostPopular</u>.
- Read the <u>ReleaseNotes</u>
- Administer this Wiki in <u>PhpWikiAdministration</u>.

<u>EditText</u> of this page (last edited December 31, 1969) [<u>info</u>] [<u>diff</u>])
<u>FindPage</u> by browsing or searching

5 best incoming links: <u>TextFormattingRules</u> (11), <u>PhpWikiAdministration</u> (7), <u>RecentChanges</u> (7), <u>ReleaseNotes</u> (7), <u>TestPage</u> (2)
5 best outgoing links: <u>AddingPages</u> (16), <u>WikiWikiWeb</u> (16), <u>HowToUseWiki</u> (14), <u>RecentVisitors</u> (12), <u>MostPopular</u> (9)
5 most popular nearby:

PostNuke

PostNuke is a CMS script and was an offshoot of PHP-Nuke with different developers and stated goals. Now the two scripts do not look or act like one another. PostNuke tends to be more secure with an improved administrative interface. It requires a MySQL database. For more information, refer to http://postnuke.com/

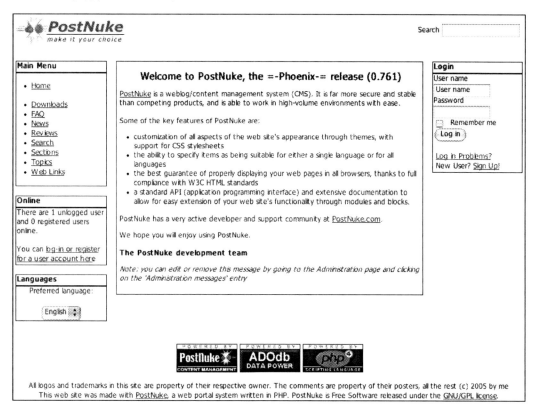

WordPress

WordPress is a popular blog script. It requires a MySQL database. For more information, refer to http://wordpress.org/.

Xoops

Xoops (pronounced *zoops*) is a CMS script. It requires a MySQL database. For more information, refer to http://xoops.org/.

Chat Rooms

Chat rooms are designed to allow many people to type messages to one another in real time. Your web host may or may not permit access to the various kinds of chat rooms that cPanel can provide. The reason for this is that chat rooms can use many server resources, especially if there are many people chatting at the same time.

cPanel offers up to three different types of chat rooms by default. Two of these chat rooms can be accessed by clicking on Chatroom from cPanel's main screen.

Entropychat

Entropychat is an HTML-based chat script. To use it you copy the displayed HTML code into the web page where you want the chat room itself to appear. You can also type a nickname into the field on this page to enter the chat room. Entropychat does not have many features. People simply enter the room and can chat with whomever is there. There are no administrative functions.

Melange

Melange is a Java-based chat program. The version cPanel offers is very old and insecure. I do not recommend that you use it. Melange is more feature-rich than Entropychat, but still does not include administrative functions. To use it, you simply access the URL displayed on the chatroom screen in cPanel. You will need to use a web browser that supports Java, however.

phpMyChat

Clicking the phpMyChat icon on the main cPanel screen accesses the most versatile of the chat scripts available in cPanel. This brings up a screen similar to the one for other Script Library scripts. You need to install it into a subdirectory of public_html. Once installed, you can also access the script via a link on this screen.

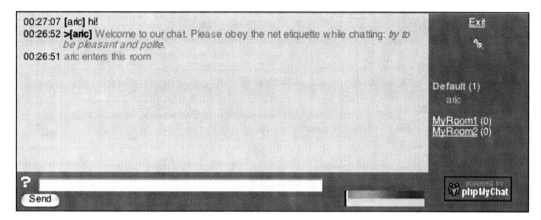

phpMyChat is written in PHP, requires an available MySQL database, and offers the most functionality of any of the chat scripts available in cPanel. It can have multiple chat rooms, administrators, moderators, private rooms, public user profiles, multiple languages, and so on.

cPanel does not, for some odd reason, offer the ability to automatically uninstall phpMyChat once it is installed. If you need to remove it you should delete the subdirectory where phpMyChat is installed and remove the database it uses from the cPanel MySQL screen (the name of the database and user you want to remove will be cpanelusername_pchat#); be sure to delete both the database and user. The link to the now non-existent installation will remain on cPanel's phpMyAdmin screen. If you would like to remove that, please contact your web host for assistance. For more information on phpMyChat, refer to http://phpmychat.sourceforge.net/.

Shopping Carts

Shopping cart scripts simplify the process of offering goods and services for purchase. These scripts support a number of different types of payment options and gateways and can make selling products on the web a lot easier. cPanel offers two different shopping carts (in addition to the Script Library osCommerce script), AgoraCart, and Interchange.

Providing detailed support for these shopping carts is beyond the scope of this book. Please visit the appropriate website (see the links below) for assistance.

AgoraCart

AgoraCart is a very flexible CGI e-commerce script. It is updated more often than osCommerce and you may find it easier to maintain. It requires a MySQL database. Unfortunately, cPanel does not automatically remove this if you install it, so you will have to remove the cart and database manually. For more information, refer to http://agoracart.com/.

Interchange

Interchange is a powerful server-side e-commerce script (that means it relies on a centrally installed server process rather than just files located in your home directory). Because of this, Interchange-based stores may not be as easy to transfer to another web host unless they also offer the same version of Interchange. Depending on your web host, they may offer version 4.8, 4.9, or 5.0 of Interchange. In addition, the developers have said that they do not support cPanel installed Interchange e-commerce scripts if you have problems. Older versions of Interchange are insecure and should be avoided. For more information, refer to http://icdevgroup.org/.

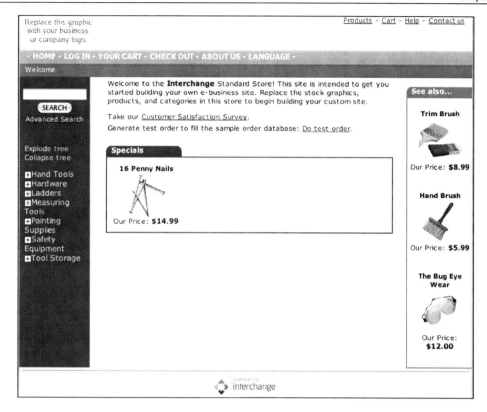

CGI Center

Your account comes with several CGI scripts installed by default. CGI stands for Common Gateway Interface. CGI scripts are usually written in Perl or Python though other programming languages like PHP can be executed as CGI also. For more information, refer to http://hoohoo.ncsa.uiuc.edu/cgi/overview.html.

CGIWrapper

This will allow you to run CGI scripts as your main cPanel user. Most web hosts already run something called suexec that automatically does the same thing as CGIWrapper, so you probably don't need to use this. Check with your web host if you are unsure. Clicking on this item will create a scgibin directory in your public_html directory. You can run CGI-BIN files from here in addition to the standard cgi-bin directory.

Random HTML

This CGI script inserts random HTML code from a list into a web page that is Server Side Includes (SSI) enabled. It comes in handy to insert placeholder text into a site you're working on, so you can see what the design looks like with content.

Simple Guestbook

If you don't want a lot of fancy features or you can't run PHP scripts or don't have any MySQL databases available then this is the guestbook for you. This allows visitors to sign comments about themselves or your website.

Advanced Guestbook

This is a link to the same Advanced Guestbook as is found in the Scripts Library.

Counter

Do you want to have a custom-designed counter to keep track of the thousands of people who will visit your site each day? Click on this item and a new window will open that will allow you to set the look and feel of the counter. You can also create a clock or countdown timer here as well. When you are done, the HTML code that you need to paste into your web page at the location where you would like the counter/clock/timer to appear will be displayed. If you want a different counter script, please look at http://hotscripts.com/ for a counter script that you like and use that instead.

Clock

Clicking this item will take you to a screen where you can set up a Java-based clock that can be displayed on any page on your website. Choose your options—click Make HTML to see a sample and to view the HTML code you need to paste into your website where you would like the clock to appear.

Countdown

This item creates a counter that counts down to a specified date and time. Setup and use is the same as for the Clock and Counter items above.

CGI E-mail

This takes input from a form on your website and e-mails it to you in an easier to read format. Those of you who have struggled with the cryptic results you get when you have forms e-mailed to you via the Web will appreciate this.

FormMail Clone

This provides the same basic service as CGI e-mail, but goes about the task slightly differently. FormMail Clone has on-line documentation, but it may not be the easiest to use. The problem with FormMail Clone is that it is very insecure and no longer actively developed. We have disabled this script on the server. Spammers use well-known flaws in this script to send out spam from your account. This is definitely a script to avoid at all costs. Use CGI E-mail or better yet, a free PHP-based form processing script from http://hotscripts.com/.

Entropy Search

This sets up an index of your website so that users can search the contents. You can also update the index for an already installed copy of Entropy Search here.

Entropy Banner

If you want to set up an advertising banner exchange program (those web ads you see at the top of many websites), you'll want to give this script a try.

Third-Party Add-ons

Your web host may also have installed a number of third-party add-ons that affect how many web scripts cPanel can install automatically for you. The most common are Netenberg.com's Fantastico, cPScripts Autoinstaller, and the Open Installer project. All of these are discussed in Chapter 12.

Finding Other Web Scripts

cPanel offers a number of web scripts, but there are hundreds of thousands more out there that you can install manually if you are feeling up to the task. There are so many scripts that finding what you need can be tricky without help.

Thankfully, many websites can help you find what you are looking for. Here are just a few:

```
http://hotscripts.com/
http://cgi.resourceindex.com/
http://scriptsearch.com/
```

Each of these sites allows you to search for scripts by description or even programming language. Once you find one you are interested in, these sites provide quick links to the author's websites, and to download links for that web script.

> Unfortunately, we do not have room in this book to cover how to manually install web scripts, especially since each script installation will be a bit different. Almost every web script comes with installation instructions or the author has installation instructions on his or her website. Be sure to read those instructions carefully to avoid installation issues.

Advice on Working with Scripts

While web scripts can allow you to do many amazing things with your website, it is imperative that you understand a few important things when working with scripts:

- If you install a web script, you must make sure that you keep it up to date. Your website is a publicly accessible resource 24 hours a day, 7 days a week, and not everyone out there is kind and friendly. There are hackers constantly trawlling the Internet looking for web scripts with security flaws that they can exploit to gain access to your entire web account or even the server itself. Making sure that you are using the latest version of the script you have installed will reduce the risk that your website will be hacked. I cannot emphasize enough just how important this is.

- The exception to the rule above is major new versions of a script that include lots of new features and functionality (for example, version 2.0 to version 3.0). Major new versions often include bugs and security issues that the developer couldn't discover in their limited testing. Wait a while to see what other people have to say about the new version. If no one complains of serious issues, feel free to upgrade.

- If you are no longer using a script, make sure you completely uninstall it. This includes removing any databases, data files, directories, and settings. Hackers cannot exploit what does not exist.

- If you use cPanel or another third-party product to install a script, you should always make sure you use it to upgrade or remove the script if possible.

- Your web host may or may not provide you any support when using web scripts. You may want to check their policy before installing any scripts. In any case, it is always a good idea to visit the developer's website to see if your questions can be answered there.

Summary

In this chapter, you learned what scripts are and what they are used for. You also discovered the many scripts that cPanel can install. Finally, you also learned some important tips about working with scripts.

10

Advanced cPanel Features

We have already covered a vast number of features that cPanel offers, but there are still more that we haven't discussed yet. So in this chapter we will explore:

- How to enable and disable FrontPage Extensions and learn why you may or may not need them
- Creating and managing add-on and parked Domains
- Creating Cron Jobs and learning what they can be used for
- The basics of working with SSH/Telnet
- Editing MIME Types and learning what they are used for
- Adding Apache Handlers and learning their uses
- The cPanel interface for creating and storing OpenPGP keys
- How to manage SSL certificates using cPanel
- The advanced Network Tools cPanel offers
- What cPanel Pro is and what new features it provides

If any of this sounds like it might be of use to you, please read on.

Welcome to cPanel 102

The various features we will be exploring in this chapter are all somewhat more advanced than we've discussed thus far. Most people can safely ignore the features mentioned here without adversely affecting their website. However, there are times when you may find that you need to avail yourself of some of the special tools that cPanel provides.

FrontPage Extensions

Microsoft FrontPage is an HTML creation program similar to Adobe GoLive, Macromedia Dreamweaver, or Contribute. To use all of the special features that FrontPage offers, your web host must allow you to have FrontPage extensions installed into your account. FrontPage will work without the server-side extensions, but some features will be disabled.

FrontPage Extensions

Warning: It is recommended that you DO NOT install FrontPage Extensions on your account unless you intend to publish your site directly from the FrontPage application.

Uninstalling the extensions from the main domain will uninstall the extensions from all subdomains and addon domains. Uninstalling will also remove all .htaccess files in your web root (public_html). You must have the extensions installed on the main domain before they can be installed on any subdomains or addon domains.

Installing or uninstalling FrontPage Extensions will result in the loss of all .htaccess files in your web area. Any directories you have protected with WebProtect will become unprotected until you reprotect them.

Domain	Status		
domain.com	not installed	(Install Extensions)	(Cleanup Old Extensions)

Clicking FrontPage Extensions in cPanel will allow you to install or remove the server-side extensions. If you are going to use FrontPage, it is a good idea to install the extensions before you do any other work on your website.

If you are not going to use FrontPage then it is recommended that you do not install the extensions (or remove them if they are already installed). If you install the FrontPage extensions and you have directories protected with the Password Protection, Hotlink, or Leech Protection features (or any other feature that relies on making changes to an .htaccess file), you will lose all of the protection and user accounts you set up. You will need to go back to the appropriate area and redefine your secure areas and users.

Add-on Domains

Add-on domains are top-level domains that you point to a subdirectory in your current web hosting account. To people visiting that domain in their web browser, it looks as if it is a totally separate website. Of course, this add-on domain shares the disk space and bandwidth limitations with your main domain, but if you have a family member or friend who wants to have their own website without all the hassle, then an add-on domain may do the trick. Not every web host permits use of add-on domains, so if you want to add one, please check with your host first.

Addon Domain Maintenance

Addon Domains are domain names that point to subdirectories within your account.

Current Addon Domains

New Domain Name: domain2.com   (www. is not needed here)

Username/directory/subdomain Name: domain2

Password: passwordhere

(Add Domain!)

Hint: This feature must be enabled for your account before you can use it. Addon Domains will not be functional unless the domain name is registered with a valid registrar and configured to point to our DNS servers.

(Setup Redirection)

(Remove Redirection)

Remove Addon Domain (Delete Domain!)

You need to make sure that the add-on domain points to your web host's **nameservers** before you add it to your account. Click Addon Domains in cPanel and add the new domain name in the specified field (without www.), create a main username/directory name/subdomain name (one name for all three, which will be created as a directory inside your public_html directory) and a password for that user. The user will be able to FTP to their web space by going to ftp.theirdomainname.com. They won't be able to access your space or log in to cPanel at their domain.

Add-on domains automatically direct hits to the directory you specified above, so you do not need to manually redirect them there. Doing so will cause errors in the visitor's web browser because you have created an infinite loop with the domain pointing repeatedly to the same location.

If you'd prefer your add-on domain to redirect people to some other location or file, you can also do that on this screen. Select the add-on domain and then click Setup Redirection. Enter the exact URL that you want to redirect to. This can be a file or some other location anywhere on the Internet. If you decide you want to remove this redirection later, you can do so by selecting the add-on domain and clicking Remove Redirection. This will cause the add-on domain to point once again to the subdirectory or subdomain you originally pointed it to when you set it up.

Finally you can completely remove an add-on domain (which you might want to do if you've decided to get that domain its own cPanel hosting account). Just select the domain and click Delete Domain.

The add-on domain feature requires cPanel to do a lot of work behind the scenes to set up or remove the domain entries and cPanel usually does a fine job. However, there may come a time when you have problems adding or removing a domain. If this happens, contact your web host so they can fix it for you.

Parked Domains

Parked domains are top-level domains that you want to point to the same content as you have available at your main domain. For example, perhaps you have `domain.com` and `domain.net` and you want someone who visits either domain to see the same content. Not every web host provides access to the Parked Domain feature. If you need it, you should contact your host for assistance.

Parked Domain Maintenance

Domain pointers allow you to "point" or "park" additional domain names to your existing hosting account. This will allow users to also reach your website when entering the "parked" or "pointed" domain into their browsers.

Current Parked Domains

New Domain Name: domain3.com   (Add Domain!)

Hint: Domains must be registered with a valid registrar before they can be parked. In addition, they will not be functional unless they are configured to point to our DNS servers.

Remove Parked Domain   [▼] (Remove Domain!)

To add a parked domain, click on Parked Domains in cPanel and enter the name of the domain (without the www.) in the New Domain Name field, then click Add Domain. To remove it, just select the parked domain from the drop-down list on this page and click Remove Domain.

> Before you attempt to add it in cPanel, make sure you point the parked domain to the same nameservers that your main domain uses.

Cron Jobs

Cron Jobs are commands or web scripts that the web server executes at a particular time. There are two different interfaces for Cron Jobs in cPanel, a UNIX-style advanced Cron manager, which is great if you know how to use Cron from a standard UNIX/Linux command line. Otherwise, you may wish to use the *Standard Cron* manager, which makes it easier to format Cron Jobs. Cron Jobs can execute any fully automated script or even some Linux commands, which makes this a very powerful feature indeed.

Cron Jobs are set to run at a certain time based on the minute, hour, day, month, and weekday given to them.

The order is always: Minute Hour Day Month Weekday Command

The hour is always set in military (24-hour) time and based on the time zone that your server is set to. Next is the day of the month you want something executed on (15 would be the 15th day of the month). Month is the month you want the Cron Job to run in (for example, 1=January and 12=December). Weekday is the day of the week you want it to run on (for example, 0=Sunday and 6=Saturday). * means to run it at every instance of this section, so a * in day would mean to run the job everyday, while a * in Minute would run the job every minute. For example, Minute = 13, Hour = 22, Day = *, Month = *, Weekday = *. This process would run everyday at 22:13, or in 12-hour format at 10:13 PM.

If you have a web script that you want to run automatically, there are several ways to do so, depending on what language the script is written in. PHP scripts can be run by typing the command php and then listing the path to the script. The script does not have to be in public_html to be run from a Cron Job. If your web host has it installed the command lynx or even wget will also execute the file. Perl scripts can be executed by typing perl and the path to the file to run.

For example, 0 1 * * * php /home/domain/cronscript.php will run the script cronscript.php at 1 AM every day, 0 1 * * * lynx /home/domain/cronscript.php would do the same thing. 0 1 * * * perl /home/domain/perlscript.pl would run the Perl script perlscript.pl at 1 AM every day.

> Running Cron Jobs too often may cause the server you are on to slow down, so be very careful about what files you run and how often you run them or you might find your account suspended by your web host.

SSH/Telnet

Clicking on this entry in your cPanel (if you have access to it) will open a Java-based terminal program that you can use to connect to any telnet or SSH server, including your own website if your web host allows it. Honestly, it is slow and not a good idea if you are going to be doing serious work. Get yourself a real SSH/Telnet client. If you want or need this feature, you probably know what it is already, and this guide would get very long indeed trying to explain all the nuances of what telnet/SSH is and how to use it. However, here are a few basics to get you started:

Telnet is a protocol for interacting remotely with a computer via a text-based interface. SSH is a secure form of telnet. It is rare that anyone uses plain telnet these days because it is so insecure.

Having SSH access will allow you to connect directly to your account on your web host's server and interact with it using standard Linux/Unix commands.

To learn more about SSH and Linux commands, visit http://ss64.com/bash/index.html. (Not all commands may work with the SSH shell that your web host provides.)

MIME Types

MIME types let a user's web browser know what a given file is so that it knows how to handle that file (display it, download it, pass it to a browser plug-in, and so on). Many common MIME types are already defined and can't be directly changed. If you have a new type of file and people are having trouble accessing it (for example, instead of downloading the file, the user's web browser tries to display the file as a text document), you may have to add a MIME type for that sort of file.

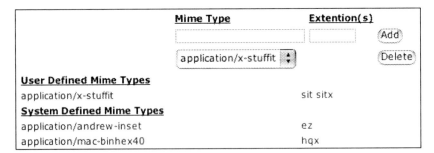

You will need to know what the MIME type should be and what **extensions** (the last 3 or 4 characters of a filename preceded by a period) the file name typically has (jpg and jpeg are both common extensions that appear on the end of JPEG picture files). Separate all extensions with a space and do not include a period.

A list of common MIME types can be found here:

`http://webmaster-toolkit.com/mime-types.shtml`

Apache Handlers

Apache handlers tell the web server itself how to handle certain types of files. You can define what the server does with certain types of files by clicking Apache Handlers in cPanel. There are a couple of handlers already installed.

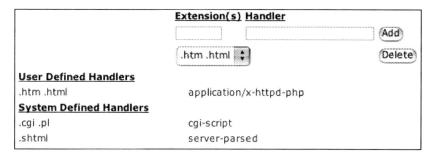

One potential use for this feature is to be able to create files that contain both HTML code and PHP code, and have both be parsed properly by Apache. Normally, if you want the code to be parsed properly you can only have PHP code in files that end in `.php`, `.php4`, or `.php3`. If you place PHP code in an `.html` file, the code will be displayed on screen as text. If you need to have both types of code in a single file, you need to tell Apache that it needs to expect PHP code in `.html` or `.htm` files. To do this, add the line Extensions: .html .htm   Handler: application/x-httpd-php. From now on, Apache will parse PHP code if it is found inside `.html` or `.htm` files.

> Be careful with Apache Handlers! Improper use could cause your website not to work properly.
>
> For more in-depth information about Apache Handlers, see the Apache documentation on the subject at `http://httpd.apache.org/docs/1.3/handler.html`.

OpenPGP Keys

PGP stands for Pretty Good Privacy and is a highly secure encryption system with public and private *keys*. You can upload your keys here if you already use PGP on your computer so that you can use those same keys to encrypt and decrypt files on your server. In addition, some scripts require the use of a PGP key to encrypt or decrypt data.

GnuPG

Public Keys:

        1024D/E00BA324 2005-12-06 admin domain (Admin) <admin@domain.com> Delete Edit

Private Keys:

        1024D/E00BA324 2005-12-06 admin domain (Admin) <admin@domain.com> Delete Edit

[Add Key] | [Import Key] | [Go Back]

In addition, there is an interface to create OpenPGP (the open-source version of PGP) keys. Click **Add Key** and fill in all of the items requested on the form that appears. The larger the key size, the more secure the resulting key will be but the longer it will take the server to generate the key. When you click **Generate Key**, be patient; this process can take time. When the key has been created, you will be informed. Once the key has been created, the main OpenPGP screen will display the cryptographic fingerprint of both the public and private keys. You can then delete the keys or edit (copy) them by clicking the appropriate word next to each key.

> Be sure to keep your private key secure and do not give it or the key password to anyone.

If you've already created keys, you can upload them also by clicking **Import Key**. Paste in a valid OpenPGP key and click **Import**. If the key is valid, it will appear on the main OpenPGP screen. If not, you will be informed of the error.

To learn more about PGP, including more about the theory behind PGP, you can visit http://pgpi.org/doc/pgpintro/, http://www.pgp.com/.

SSL Management

SSL stands for Secure Socket Layer (also sometimes referred to as TLS or Transport Layer Security) and it is the main protocol used on the Web to ensure that traffic to and from a website is encrypted so third parties cannot intercept data (like your credit card information). SSL is important if you are accepting payments on your website. You don't want the private information your customers send you to be intercepted by hackers. Many people will refuse to submit financial or other private information to a website that doesn't offer SSL.

To learn more about how SSL works, visit http://computer.howstuffworks.com/encryption4.htm.

In order to use SSL to encrypt traffic to and from your website you need an SSL certificate. There are a wide variety of SSL certificates and certificate providers. Some certificates cost as little as 30 USD a year and some as much as 4,000 USD a year. What makes these certificates different from one another, and which one do you need? These questions and more can be answered at http://whichssl.com/.

Your web host may require that you purchase your SSL certificate from them, so you may want to check with them before buying anything.

> You will definitely need a **dedicated IP address** (an IP address assigned only to your domain) if you plan to have an SSL certificate installed. If your web hosting account did not come with a dedicated IP address (which it probably did not) you will need to obtain one. Contact your web host for assistance.

In order to buy an SSL certificate, you will need to send the provider some information about you, your website, and the server on which the website is hosted. The *SSL Manager* feature in cPanel helps you create the information that you can then provide to the company from whom you are buying your SSL certificate. Once you have a certificate, you can use the SSL Manager to install it.

> An improperly generated certificate request or improperly installed certificate could cause problems for your website or cost you more money (because you need to get the certificate reissued) so I strongly recommend that you talk with your web host before attempting to use cPanel's SSL Manager features. Your web host will probably be happy to handle the entire process for you from start to finish.

Once you know what kind of certificate you need, you will need to generate an SSL key first. This key is used to encrypt data exclusively for your website. Click Private Keys (KEY) to generate a site key.

SSL Manager

SSL Keys

Keys on Server

No SSL KEYs Found

Upload a New Key

Paste the key below:

or Choose a .key file: (Browse...)

Key Domain:

(Upload) *

* It is recommended that you upload the Certificate (.crt) file first so it can be matched with the Key (.key) file.

Generate a New Key

Host   <- (Select a Domain) [↕]

(Generate)

View

[↕] (Show)

Delete

[↕] (Delete) *

* Deleting a key will remove the Certificate Signing Request (CSR) and Certificate (CRT) if it exists.

If you already have a key installed, then you will see it displayed here. Do not create a new key for the same domain or subdomain if you already have one installed unless you know you need it (and be sure to remove the old key first). If you have a key file already generated locally that you want to use, paste the key content into the box on this screen, or select the .KEY file from your computer to upload it to your account.

If you do not have a key at all, you need to generate one. Doing so is simple. Type in the domain or subdomain name that you will want to secure with an SSL certificate in the Host field on this page (or just select one from the drop-down menu next to this field) then click the Generate button to create a key.

You may need to provide this key to your web host or SSL certificate provider. If so, you can choose the key from drop-down list under the View heading and clicking Show.

If you want to remove an SSL certificate from your account, you can remove the key it uses. Select the key from the drop-down menu under the Delete heading and click Delete. Both the .KEY and .CRT files will be removed when you do this.

Once you've created a key for the domain or subdomain you want to secure, click Certificate Signing Requests (CSR) to create one. This CSR file will definitely need to be given to the SSL certificate provider so they can create your SSL certificate. The information you enter here must match exactly the information you give your SSL certificate provider. Depending on the type of certificate you are requesting, they may double-check the information you provide them to make sure it is a real person and company. Do not forget any of the information you enter in the CSR, especially not the password, since that password will be needed to install your final certificate. Make sure you generate the CSR for the correct host (domain or subdomain). If you make mistakes, delete the certificate using the Delete feature on this page. Once you've successfully created a CSR you can also view it on this page.

SSL Manager

SSL Certificate

Certificates on Server

No SSL CRTs Found

Upload a New Certificate

Paste the crt below:

or Choose a .crt file: [   ] (Browse...)
(Upload)

Generate a New Certificate

Host   [ ] *
Country   [ ]
State   [   ]
City   [   ]
Company   [   ]
Company Divison [   ]
Email   [   ]
(Generate)

* You must generate or upload a key before you can generate any certificates.

View

[ ] (Show)

Delete

[ ] (Delete)

The final step after you've purchased the certificate and received the .CRT and perhaps a .CA (Certificate Authority) file is to install the certificate on your server. Clicking **Certificates (CRT)** in cPanel's SSL Manager will allow you to do this. You can either paste the .CRT file contents in to the box on this page or select your .CRT file from your local computer and upload it. Once you've done that, assuming the key and CSR match exactly the CRT, you should be able to access pages securely on that domain or subdomain by visiting https://domain.com/.

If you get any errors, please double-check your key, CSR, and CRT files to make sure they are correct. If you can't figure out what is wrong, please contact your web host for assistance.

It is possible to create self-signed SSL certificates from the CRT screen in cPanel. In that case, the web server itself creates a certificate you can use for secure transactions. Self-signed certificates will always produce a warning any time a user tries to access a secure page (at least one time per browsing session) on your website since the self-signed certificate is not from a trusted source. I do not recommend you try to create or use one. Some providers like http://godaddy.com/, offer SSL certificates for 30 USD or less per year, so it is better to spend a little money to get a real certificate.

Network Tools

For slightly more advanced users, this section provides a quick interface to a couple of common network tools (domain lookup and trace route).

Domain Lookup Tool

Domain lookup will return the IP address for whatever domain you type in to this location as well as basic information about the domain (from the DNS zone). If the domain you are looking up is not on the same server as your account, the information returned will be quite limited (just the IP address that the domain is using).

```
DNS Results:

domain.com has address 111.111.111.111




Zone Information:

domain.com name server ns1.domain.com
domain.com name server ns2.domain.com
domain.com has address 111.111.111.111
ftp.domain.com has address 111.111.111.111
localhost.domain.com has address 127.0.0.1
secure.domain.com has address 111.111.111.111
www.secure.domain.com has address 111.111.111.111
```

Traceroute Tool

Traceroute lists the route your data would take between your computer and the domain that you type in. Each stop on the trip will list the response time (**ping**) from each server in milliseconds (ms). Lower numbers are better, high numbers mean your connection may be adversely affected. You may be able to get complete results from `http://dnsstuff.com/`.

The only problem with using a site like this is that the trace route is listed from their servers to the destination. If you want to see the route between your current location (perhaps, your home computer) and the destination server, you need to run Traceroute from your current location.

On PCs running Windows, you can go to the Start | Run option and then type:

`tracert domain name or IP address`

On a Macintosh, running Mac OS X, go to Applications/Utilities and then double-click on Terminal. At the command prompt, type:

`traceroute domain name or IP address`

For Linux or Unix, the process is similar to Mac OS X (since Mac OS X is based on OpenBSD), just drop to your favorite shell command line if you aren't there already and type in the same command as above.

cPanel Pro

Despite the name, cPanel Pro isn't a new or special version of cPanel, though if your web host has activated it, you will likely have access to a few extra features. cPanel Pro is designed to make it easier for third-party developers to add new features to cPanel. Prior to cPanel Pro, it was very difficult for a developer to add new features to cPanel since these features would often be removed whenever cPanel was updated. This made it very hard for web hosts to offer extra features to help enhance their service. cPanel Pro gives developers an easier way to incorporate new features that won't break every time cPanel is updated. To show developers how to write cPanel Pro modules, cPanel Inc. provides several new features along with the sample code showing how the feature is implemented. For the end user this means you may have access to several extra features. cPanel Inc. has moved a couple of features (Stats Select and BoxTrapper) from cPanel Pro add-on modules to standard cPanel options, so it may be that even if your web host doesn't offer cPanel Pro features yet you will see these in some future version of cPanel.

Image Manager

This feature uses ImageMagick to help you accomplish several image-related tasks. You can create thumbnails (small preview pictures) of a graphic image or even an entire directory full of images. Each image will have a separate generated thumbnail. You can use the thumbnail as a *preview* of the full-size image, saving download time while allowing your visitors to get a sense of what the image looks like. You can scale an image up or down in size (perhaps to make it fit better on the average monitor). Lastly, you can convert one image or a directory of images to a different format supported by ImageMagick.

If you would like more information on ImageMagick, and how it works, please visit the developer's website: `http://imagemagick.org/`.

```
Image Manager

Thumbnailer

        Select a Directory

Image Scaler

        Select a File

Convert Image Format (jpg,gif,bmp,etc)

        Select a Directory or File
```

Leech Protect

This feature helps control access to password-protected areas of your website. It ensures that a user cannot give their login information to lots of other people and thus steal your revenue. It does this by monitoring users' logins and disabling any login that is used more than a set number of times in two hours. This feature is discussed more fully in Chapter 6.

ClamAV

This provides you with the ability to scan the files and mail in your cPanel account with ClamAV `http://clamav.net/`, a free and constantly updated virus scanner. This feature is discussed more in Chapter 4.

Submit a Support Request

This link is a convenience. Clicking it will take you to your web host's help desk or allow you to send an e-mail to your host if you are experiencing any problems or have questions about your hosting account.

Support Request Submit

From   admin@domain.com   Change Default
Subject I have a question about cPanel
Body   How does the Submit Support Request feature work?

        Regards,

        Thadeus Snaverly III
        Administrator

Send

Summary

In this chapter, you learned how to use a wide variety of advanced features found in cPanel. You've discovered how to install and remove Microsoft FrontPage extensions, add add-on and parked domains, work with Cron Jobs and SSH, manage OpenPGP keys and SSL certificates, and use network tools and cPanel Pro features.

In the next chapter, we will cover a very important topic: security. I recommend that everyone read Chapter 11 carefully, because failing to follow the suggestions there could put not only your own account data in jeopardy, but also all accounts on the entire server.

11

Site and Account Security

This is probably the most important topic covered in this book. Following the recommendations in this chapter will enable you to avoid serious problems. However, if the worst does happen, you'll also find an action plan that will help you to get your account up and running again quickly while helping you to avoid the same problem(s) in the future. Specifically, we will cover the following:

- What hacking is and why you may be at risk
- What you can do to protect yourself and your site from attack
- What to do if your site is hacked

First, we'll explore why everyone with a web presence needs to take security precautions.

Site Security and You

You have or will have shortly a presence on the Internet available to anyone 24 hours a day, 7 days a week. While this constant availability is great for business, it also means that those with less-than-pure intentions can try to disrupt your site at any time.

Depending on who you talk to, individuals who attempt to disrupt websites and computer systems illegally might be called hackers, black hat hackers, crackers, or even script kiddies (less proficient individuals who rely on well-known security issues and more commonly available hacking tools). In this book, I will refer to them all as hackers.

You may be thinking, "No one would bother messing with my little website devoted to pictures of my dog." Think again! You may not have credit card information or other private data stored in your account, but that won't stop a hacker who decides they want to mess with your site. The simple fact that your site is available 24/7 on the Internet is a big draw. In addition, some hackers deface websites just to show off their hacking skills—*just because they can.*

What harm can hackers do? Here are just a few things that could happen:

- **The hacker uses an insecure form mail script on your site to send spam and viruses from your account.** Your domain and perhaps even the entire web server are placed on mail blacklists and you have problems sending legitimate mail to others in the future. In addition, you have to deal with angry requests to stop sending spam and deal with potentially thousands of e-mail bounce messages for mail sent to addresses that do not exist.

- **A program is uploaded to your website and uses your web server to attack other sites.** This can severely slow down all of the websites hosted on your server as well as get your server placed on more blacklists.

- **The hacker is able to run a secret meeting place for his friends and other hackers right from your website.** Not only will this probably slow down your server, but it also puts other accounts on your server at risk as more hackers explore looking for other vulnerable sites.

- **Your website and all of the data it contains can be destroyed, defaced, stolen, or tampered with.** In fact, it is possible for hackers to use one hacked account on a shared server to gain access to other accounts or even the entire server (though their ability to do so depends in part on how your web host has the server configured).

- **Your website itself or the entire server could be attacked, keeping people from being able to visit it.** This can be done without compromising the data in your account and can be very difficult to stop once it starts. Your web host will need to assist you.

As you can see, even a small site is a tempting draw. While your web host can help protect the server your account is hosted on, it will primarily be up to you to keep your site out of the hands of hackers.

The Security Plan

What can you do to protect yourself and your website(s) from hacker attacks? First the bad news: If a hacker really wants to get into your website or take your site off the Web, then he or she can probably do so (given enough time and effort) and you can't do much about it. After all, if a hacker can break into the FBI or CIA website and cause problems, what chance do you have?

Don't panic! There are some basic steps that you can take to help guard against anyone gaining illegal access to your site and to help you get back up and running again if the worst really does happen. As the saying goes:

"Hope for the best, plan for the worst, and expect anything in between."

Here are some common ways that hackers gain access to your site (or even your home computer) in no particular order:

- **Weak Passwords**: While using a short, simple password at every Internet site you access (and at your own website) may make life somewhat easier for you, it also makes breaking into your site nearly child's play for a hacker. A small note pad or notebook and pen or pencil will probably cost you very little, but it can make it simultaneously much easier for you to remember what complex password you used at a given website and also that much harder for a hacker to gain access to your private information. Use different usernames and passwords on every website you access and keep a log of them all. Don't use simple passwords that are words. Make sure the password contains letters and numbers, and *ChAnGe ThE CaSe* if the site password is case sensitive. Do not write the passwords themselves in the book, in case you lose it. Write a *hint* to yourself that you know will make it easy for you to reconstruct the correct password. For example, if your password is *MHirvg79*, then you might write something like this as a hint: "*My Host is really very good + the year of my birth*". This is rather simple, but you can get the general idea from it. There are also several computer programs that offer to save passwords and other sensitive information in a heavily encrypted format so only if a person knows the (hopefully hard to guess) master password will they be able to access your private info, even if they steal the file itself. A few of these programs are listed in Chapter 13. In addition, you should also remember to change your password regularly by using the Change Password feature in cPanel discussed in Chapter 6.

Ideally, you should not write down your passwords at all; you should memorize them and never tell them to anyone else. However, unless you have a photographic memory, this is unlikely to be feasible without relying on just a few passwords. It is more secure to follow my suggestions above than risk using just a few simple passwords. Just be sure to keep your password book or program well protected!

- **Insecure Scripts/Programs**: Although that new script you found might be the best thing since the advent of the Internet, that doesn't mean that it is totally secure. Hackers constantly look for *holes* that will allow them to bypass the security built into a script or program and the more popular a script is, the more likely that hackers will target it to try to find holes. Once you make a choice to install a script or program on your website (whether you use cPanel's Scripts Library or install the script manually), it will be up to you to make sure that you keep up with installing the latest versions of a script. New versions of scripts don't just add new features; they very often fix identified security holes. If you are uncertain how to go about updating the scripts you use, ask other people who use the same script or visit the website of the author(s) of the script in question and see if they have directions on how to upgrade from an older version. Chances are good that they will be able to help.

- **Social Engineering**: Unbelievably, hackers can often gain access to your site directly from you. They might send you an e-mail claiming to be someone from your web host or some other official-sounding company. They may tell you that you need to go to a particular web page and update your personal information or enter your credit card information. The website might even look legitimate on the surface. How do you defend against this sort of thing? First, pay attention to what information you are being asked for. Does it make sense? Does the e-mail address, URL, and so on not match what you think it should? For example, if your web host doesn't provide support via instant messaging clients and all of the sudden you get an instant message from someone claiming to be from them, be very careful and don't give out any personal information. Immediately contact the company through official channels and find out if the contact is really from an employee or not. Most companies are very careful about this and will only contact you through official channels. Keep in mind that most web hosts use a payment processor like PayPal or 2checkout.com to handle credit card and payment options and so should never need access to your personal credit card information (though they may ask for the last 4 digits for verification). Check with your host when in doubt and do not provide personal or financial information to anyone you don't know. Even if you are sure that the company or person contacting you is who they say they are and they have a legitimate need for information, do not provide them with more information than they absolutely need.

- **Virus/Worm/Keylogger/Spyware**: If you don't have a good virus-scanning program, then you really should go out and get one right now (a few are listed in Chapter 13). Also, be sure to keep it up to date or it will be useless. Even if you have one that is up to date, don't allow this to lull you into a false sense of security; new viruses, and other security threats are released nearly every day, so it's possible your virus scanner could miss the very latest virus/worm or keylogger. In addition, you need to be careful not to let that *friend of a friend* have unsupervised access to your computer, no matter how nice they seem. It only takes a few seconds for a prepared hacker to install a nearly invisible keylogger that records everything you type and sends a copy to the person who installed it. They can use that to gain access to all of your personal information.

These are not the only ways that a hacker can gain access to your site or computer, but they are some of the most common.

Another common type of attack is a Denial of Service (**DOS**) attack. This sort of attack uses many computers to flood your web server with fake requests for information. While this won't affect the data in your account like a direct hacking attempt could, it will slow down your server to the point where your website may no longer be accessible. Web hosts and data centers work hard to combat these sorts of attacks, but they are difficult to protect against. Please try to be understanding with your host if your server is the subject of a DOS attack, because it can take a while to filter out all of the *fake* traffic and return things to normal. Rather than go into depth here about exactly how DOS attacks work, please read the article at `http://grc.com/dos/drdos.htm`, which explains it quite well.

I hope that you will never experience such an attack, but if you do, at least you will know exactly what is happening.

What to do if the Worst Happens

OK, now it's time for the *plan for the worst* part—what should you do if your site is hacked?

Step One: Contact Your Web Host

Remember, don't panic! The damage is probably already done and isn't likely to get much worse (if you act quickly). Try to stay calm and provide your web host with as much information as you can, not necessarily limited to but including:

- The domain name of the site that has been hacked, with a URL to a page illustrating the problem if possible.

- Your cPanel username and your server's IP address (or the server name if you know it). You can typically find the server IP address in the welcome account information that your web host sent you (you should never delete this information).

- Your host will probably need to confirm that you are the legitimate owner of the site. Receiving an e-mail or call from you isn't necessarily good proof that you are who you say you are (as these can be spoofed). Your web host may ask you for your billing information like the name on the account, the billing address, last 4 digits of your credit card (but be wary if someone asks for the entire number), the plan you originally signed up for, when you signed up, or even a *secret question* that you provided an answer to when you first signed up. Try to make sure you have as much of this information as possible on hand before you contact your host.

- You should provide as much information about the problem as you can manage: When did you first notice the problem? Did someone threaten to hack your site recently? Did you receive any threatening or odd e-mails either before or after your site was hacked? Did you notice anything odd in your site error log or raw web logs in the days or hours leading up to the attack? If you don't know exactly when the hacking attempt happened, when was the last time you accessed your site and it worked fine?

Your web host should be able to provide you some additional information concerning how your site was hacked, so be sure to ask them to investigate this incident thoroughly. Your host will likely do this anyway, since it is in their own best interest, but it's always good to ask just to be safe.

It is important to learn from any hacking experience so that you do everything in your power not to fall prey to the same kind of attack again. Hopefully, this will never happen to you, but if it does it is always helpful to be prepared.

Step Two: Restore and Verify All Data and Secure Site

Once the hacker has been locked out of your account and your site returns to your control you should change any site or account passwords so you can be sure that hackers will not have access to anything in your account. Then it is time to assess the damage and try to restore your files. Did you have any important private information on your site? (Credit card information, information about your personal addresses, private mail, passwords, and so on.) You may want to contact your credit card company or any other users who might have been affected and let them know what happened so they can take steps to protect both you and themselves.

It is possible that your host has backups of your files from before the hacking attempt, but you should not count on this. Having your own recent backup is critical. Hence, it is a good idea to keep more than one previous backup; if you don't notice the problem until after your next scheduled backup you will still have something you can use. Even if your host does have a recent backup, it may take time for them to locate your files and restore them for you. Having your own backup will make sure you are up and running as quickly as possible.

Restore your account data from your own backups that you made using cPanel's backup feature (or any other backup method that you used). Just log into your cPanel account and restore the home directory backup, e-mail aliases, filters, and MySQL databases. If you have taken a full site backup through cPanel, you will need to upload this backup to your home directory and ask your web host to restore it for you. If you used other methods to backup the data in your account, you will probably need to manually copy the backup files into place over the current ones (be sure to remove any files you don't recognize from your site, as the hacker may have added them).

Never trust that any file on your website wasn't modified in some malicious way. Even scripts and databases that seem to be intact and working may have been altered somehow. Good hackers are quite subtle because they don't want you to realize your site has been compromised and thus take steps to lock them out. Leaving hacked content in place could make it easier for the hacker to gain access to your account again. Pay special attention to any .htaccess files in your public_html directory or subdirectories and custom error .shtml files (404.shtml). These files may be modified in such a way that even if other content isn't modified, visitors may be redirected to other websites or messages from the hackers.

Update any scripts you use on your website to the latest version. If you know that a hacker has got access to your site via an insecure script and that script does not have a more recent update, you should consider disabling it until one comes out or switching to another, more secure script.

In addition, look carefully in your entire account for any suspicious files that weren't there before your site was hacked. If you've manually uploaded files back to your web account from a backup, you may be leaving some new (hacked) files in place. If you see something that seems suspicious, remove the files and report the find to your web host, providing a sample if requested. They should be able to tell you if the files are anything to worry about or if they are required for proper site operation. Such files may also provide your web host with more information about who hacked your account and how it was done.

Once your site is clean and working properly again, watch your web stats and error logs for additional unusual behavior because hackers will usually revisit your website to see if they can gain access to your data again. Report anything that seems odd to your web host immediately.

If you or your web host have determined what IP address or addresses the hacker used to access your website, you may be tempted to place them in your IP ban list in cPanel (discussed in Chapter 6). While this isn't a bad thing, keep in mind that most hackers can easily switch IP addresses and the IP banning tool in cPanel only prevents website (port 80) access by that IP address. It doesn't stop FTP, e-mail, cPanel or other types of access. In addition, if you block a wide range of IP addresses you risk blocking legitimate traffic to your site. Your web host (if they wish) can ban an IP or range of IPs from ever accessing anything on the entire server.

Summary

In this chapter, you learned why even the smallest website could be a big target for hackers. You also learned to help protect yourself by creating secure passwords, keeping your web scripts updated, maintaining regular backups, and watching for suspicious activity. If the worst happens and your site is hacked, you've learned that you need to contact your web host immediately, and what sort of information you need to provide them when you do. Once your site is back under your control you know how to restore and verify the data in your account and what steps to take to prevent this from ever happening again.

In the next chapter, we will explore many popular themes and add-ons for cPanel.

12

Third-Party Additions to cPanel

As impressive as the many default features of cPanel are, many web hosts try to differentiate their hosting packages by adding a new look or new features to their plans. This chapter will cover most common cPanel additions, and you will discover:

- Many popular cPanel themes and learn about what makes them unique
- A number of popular third-party add-ons for cPanel and learn how they work

cPanel Themes: New Look, New Features

cPanel **themes** provide a new look and feel for cPanel and may also add new features not typically available in cPanel's default XSkin theme. The screenshots in this guide show the XSkin theme. Although many web hosts use the XSkin theme because it is cPanel's default theme and is constantly updated to support all of cPanel's features, there are hosts that choose to use a different theme in order to provide enhanced features or distinguish their hosting plans from other hosts.

Since some hosts use the themes exclusively it is important that you see what they look like and what, if any, special features they offer compared to cPanel's default XSkin theme. Keep in mind that not all themes support all third-party add-ons or all cPanel features.

cPanel's Other Themes

Although cPanel's default theme is XSkin, it isn't the only theme cPanel Inc. offers for free with cPanel. These themes are not updated as often as XSkin but allow hosts some different choices without forcing them to pay a third party.

Blue Lagoon

Blue Lagoon looks similar to the various Xskin themes except that it uses fewer graphics and so will load faster than XSkin. It supports cPanel Pro and many third-party add-ons.

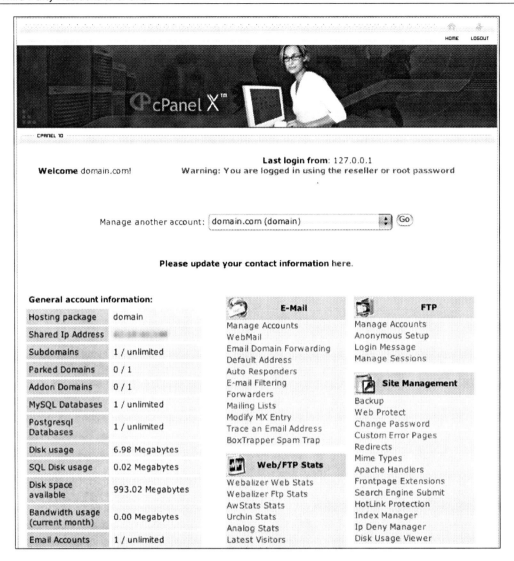

Each major section of features has a single graphic followed by a plain text link to each feature. Blue Lagoon has been around for many years, though it used to look very different in the past. For example, the header of this theme used to be similar to the one that was used by XSkin.

Monsoon

Monsoon is another theme that is light on graphics. It is the most recent theme added by cPanel Inc. and it requires cPanel 8.4.0E96 or later. It incorporates some of the look of the old-style Blue Lagoon theme along with modern cPanel features.

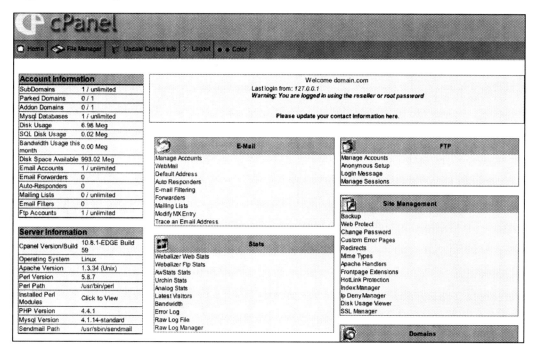

Monsoon supports cPanel Pro and many third-party add-ons. It also comes in two colors, blue (which is more gray than blue) and red (which is more pink than red). Clicking on one of the colors in the header allows the user to switch between them at will.

Xmail

Xmail is a theme based on XSkin except that it only offers the user e-mail-related features.

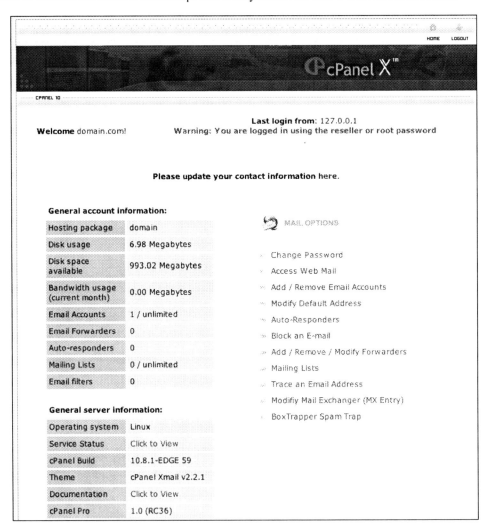

Xmail does not support cPanel Pro or any third-party add-ons. However, you do have the ability to access all e-mail-related features including forwarders, web mail, auto-responders, and so on.

X2

X2 is an alternative form of cPanel's standard XSkin theme. It looks almost the same as XSkin.

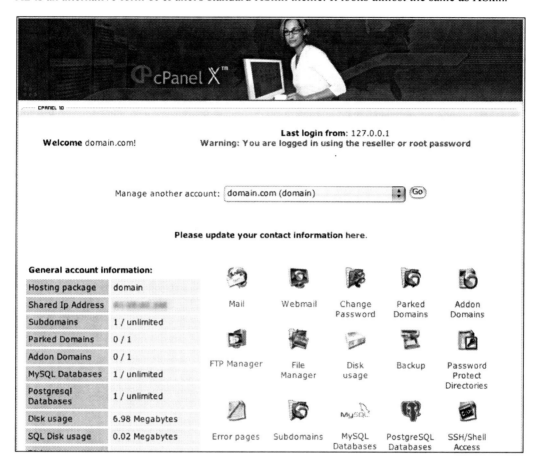

X2 supports cPanel Pro and many third-party add-ons. X2 removes some information from the standard XSkin theme that some web hosts don't like to offer to clients.

Third-Party Themes

Since cPanel Inc. does not provide many themes with cPanel and since themes are not easy for web hosts to create, many other companies have stepped up to provide themes that not only change the look of cPanel but in some cases also add new features not available in cPanel's own themes. What follows is a discussion of all of the actively supported themes that I have been able to find, listed in alphabetical order. There may be others and your web host may have created their own themes.

7Dana

Publisher: 7Dana (http://7dana.com/)

Supports: cPanel Pro

Special Features: Sidebar with collapsible tree of links to cPanel features

7Dana is a free cPanel theme released on cPanel.net's support forum. This theme has a center bank of icons like XSkin but it also has collapsible tree of links to every feature in the sidebar. Information about your account appears at the bottom of the screen.

Ace

Publisher: cpSkins (http://cpskins.com/)

Supports: cPanel Pro, some third-party add-ons

Special Features: Theme changer (cpSkins themes only), fast loading, support for multiple languages

Ace is a clean primarily white theme with few graphics (except the header). As with most cpSkins themes, your web host can enable a theme switcher that will allow you to choose from other cpSkins themes.

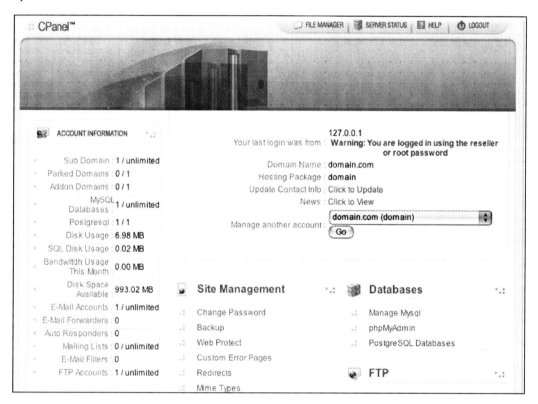

BlueCrush

Publisher: cpSkins (http://cpskins.com/)

Supports: cPanel Pro, some third-party add-ons

Special Features: Theme changer (cpSkins themes only), fast loading, support for multiple languages

This is one of the few dark cPanel themes available. It doesn't have many graphics and supports the cpSkins theme changer.

CoolBreeze

Publisher: Netenberg (http://netenberg.com/)

Supports: cPanel Pro, Fantastico

Special Features: Fast loading, support for multiple languages

This is another theme that is designed to be quick loading and focused on providing every link and piece of information you need on one, easy-to-read screen.

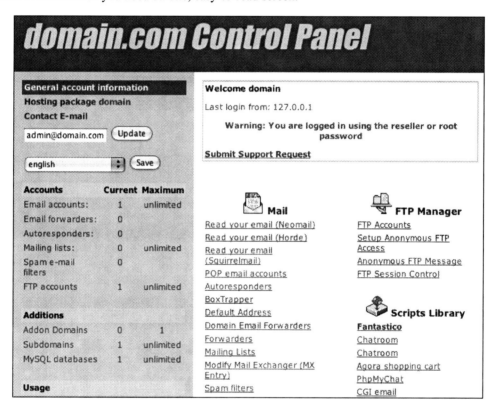

CPANEL XP Evolution

Publisher: CpanelSkinDepot (http://cpanelskindepot.com/)

Supports: cPanel Pro, some third-party add-ons

Special Features: Theme changer (CPANEL XP Evolution and XSkin and X2 themes only), customizable by host and resellers, tool tips (optional), flash tutorial integration

CPANEL XP Evolution (Evo) is a theme that is reminiscent of the default blue theme for Microsoft Windows® XP. It also tries to extend cPanel in a number of ways. It supports a wide variety of languages, is completely customizable by web hosts and their resellers via a special web application called CPAPP, includes a basic help desk feature, and integrates with a number of third-party products and scripts.

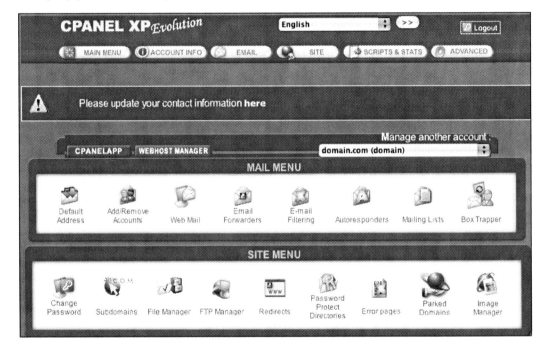

cpSkins

Publisher: cpSkins (http://cpskins.com/)

Supports: cPanel Pro, some third-party add-ons

Special Features: Theme changer (cpSkins themes only), quick loading, many theme colors, direct web mail login from the main screen, support for multiple languages

cpSkins is designed to be quick loading while allowing the user to choose from a number of different colors for the interface.

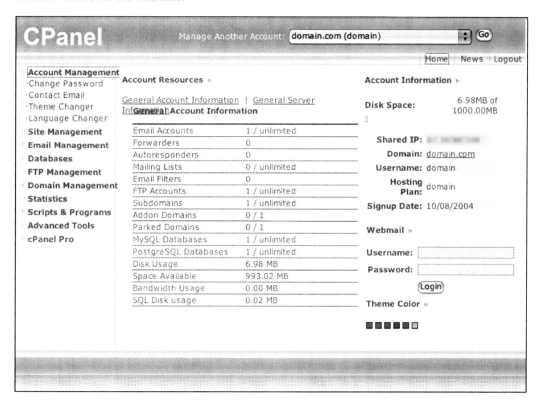

iCandy

Publisher: cpSkins (http://cpskins.com/)

Supports: cPanel Pro, some third-party add-ons

Special Features: Theme changer (cpSkins themes only), support for multiple languages

This theme is designed to look nice without worrying about the time it takes to load in the user's web browser. The icons are rather playful and those on broadband connections probably won't mind the additional loading time.

InteliSkin

Publisher: cpSkins (http://cpskins.com/)

Supports: cPanel Pro, some third-party add-ons

Special Features: Theme changer (cpSkins themes only), support for multiple languages, quick loading

This theme is designed to be quick loading and provide every link you need on a single screen.

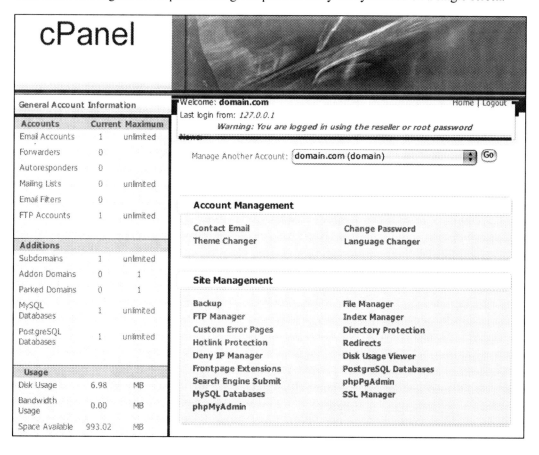

Java

Publisher: PixelByPixel (http://pixelbypixel.com/)

Supports: Fantastico

Special Features: Theme changer (PixelByPixel themes only)

This theme is designed to be very good looking. It unfortunately does not support cPanel Pro or most third-party add-ons. It includes a theme changer to switch between the two currently released PixelByPixel cPanel themes (Java and Winterfall).

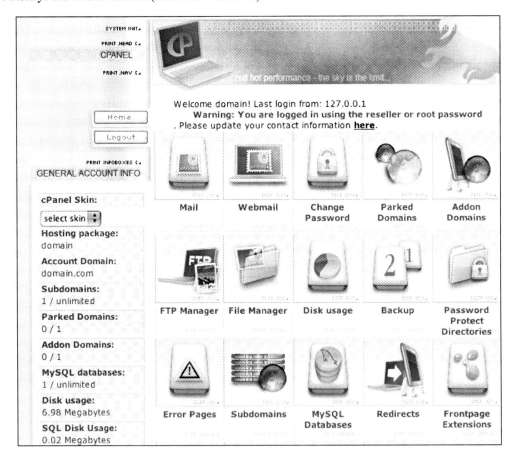

Radiance

Publisher: cpSkins (http://cpskins.com/)

Supports: cPanel Pro, some third-party add-ons

Special Features: Theme changer (cpSkins themes only), support for multiple languages, custom login screen

This theme is designed to make it easy to find and access all the features and information cPanel provides from a single screen. Your host can also install a special login screen so that cPanel's standard *please log in* screen looks like this theme.

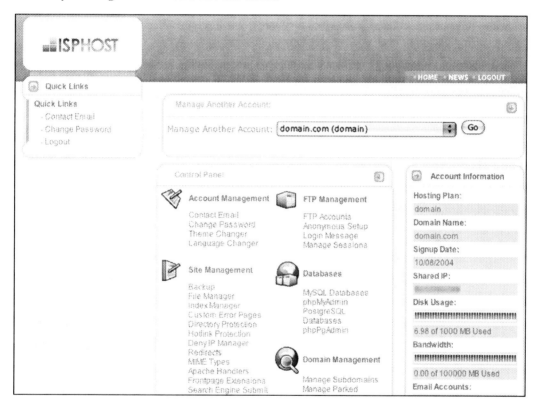

RVSKIN

Publisher: RVSKIN (http://rvskin.com/)

Supports: cPanel Pro, all third party add-ons that follow cPanel Pro guidelines

Special Features: Theme changer (RVSKIN themes only), support for multiple languages, every item is customizable by both web hosts and resellers, sub-reseller feature, up-sell feature, integration with nearly any item through custom pages and links, complete control over every offered feature by resellers, updated constantly to work with all recent versions of cPanel, custom themes

RVSKIN was created to allow web hosts and resellers as much flexibility as possible while still supporting via regular automated updates every new feature cPanel adds. RVSKIN isn't just a set of themes, it is an entire cPanel management system. Resellers love RVSKIN because they can customize any feature or even add entirely new links or pages to cPanel.

RVSKIN permits **up-selling**. Up-selling allows a web host or reseller to place links in cPanel to features that won't work until the user pays for them. RVSKIN integrates with your billing software to allow a user to pay for additional features, space, bandwidth, and so on right from cPanel.

Sub-reselling allows resellers to offer basic reseller plans of their own using RVSKIN. The features sub-resellers have are somewhat limited compared to the standard cPanel/WHM reseller interface, but it works as advertised.

Support for many languages is another strongpoint for RVSKIN. It offers true multilingual support for almost every item in the cPanel interface. Resellers and web hosts can easily add their own languages if they wish and even post news in multiple languages (that gets displayed depending on the user's language preference).

RVSKIN is currently the only theme to provide automated support for both cPanel Pro's default features and any third-party add-on that conforms to cPanel Inc.'s standards.

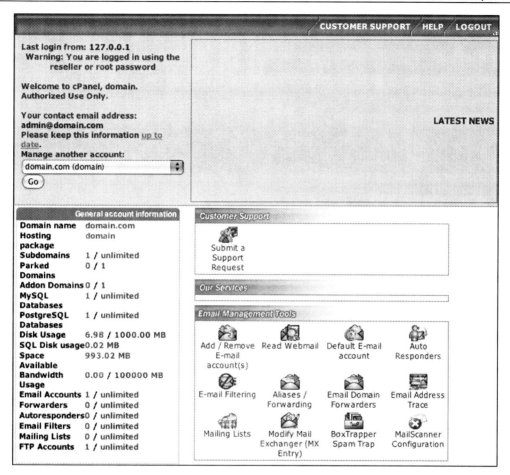

Simskins

Publisher: cpSkins (http://cpskins.com/)

Supports: cPanel Pro, some third-party add-ons

Special Features: Theme changer (cpSkins themes only), support for multiple languages, quick loading, many user-selectable colors

SimSkins is another largely text-only cPanel theme. It supports multiple languages, cpSkins theme changer and even multiple theme colors.

Stainless Steel

Publisher: Netenberg (http://netenberg.com/)

Supports: cPanel Pro, Fantastico

Special Features: Support for multiple languages, quick-loading

A dark-colored quick-loading theme.

Trix

Publisher: cpSkins (http://cpskins.com/)

Supports: cPanel Pro, some third-party add-ons

Special Features: Theme changer (cpSkins themes only), support for multiple languages, multiple colors, web mail login from main page

This theme is designed to be clean while still offering many graphic elements. The user can quickly switch between colors at will. Trix also comes in an e-mail-only version for users that purchase e-mail-only plans.

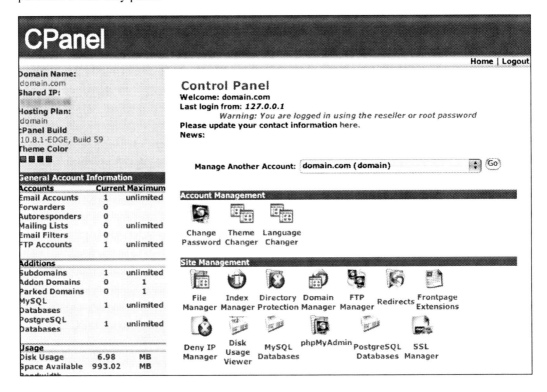

Winterfall

Publisher: PixelByPixel (http://pixelbypixel.com/)

Supports: Fantastico

Special Features: Theme changer (PixelByPixel themes only)

Winterfall is designed to be clean looking but graphic rich. Users can switch at will between the two currently released PixelByPixel cPanel themes, Java and Winterfall.

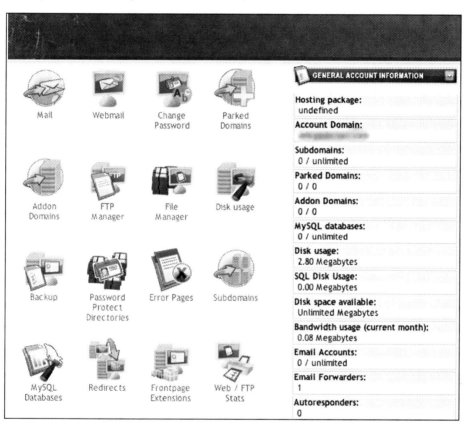

XController

Publisher: Netenberg (http://netenberg.com/)

Supports: cPanel Pro, Fantastico

Special Features: Support for multiple languages

XController is designed to look similar to Mac OS X. It supports cPanel Pro features and Fantastico as well as several languages. Later in 2006, XController will be replaced with Universina, which will have the ability to be themed so it can look like anything you want (though it will look like XController by default). In addition, Universina will add several features not found currently in other cPanel themes. Anyone with a valid XController license will be able to upgrade to Universina for free.

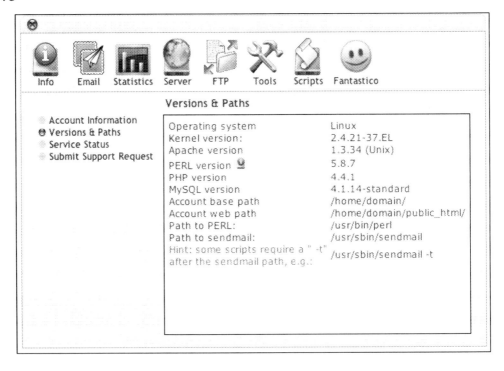

ZabrinskiPoint

Publisher: Netenberg (`http://netenberg.com/`)

Supports: cPanel Pro, Fantastico

Special Features: Quick-loading

A bright, mostly text theme designed to be quick loading. It supports cPanel Pro features and Fantastico.

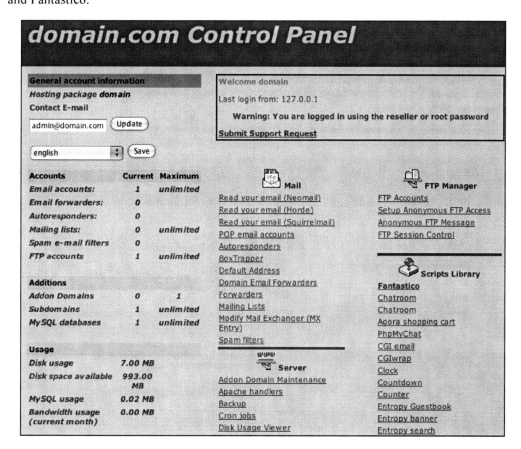

Third-Party Add-ons

A few companies have also chosen to offer new feature add-ons for cPanel. In the past, this was not an easy thing. However, since cPanel now has made it easier for others to add new features with the advent of cPanel Pro, there has been an upsurge in third-party add-ons.

It isn't possible to discuss every third-party add-on in this book, but the most common add-ons deserve a mention since your host may offer them.

Fantastico: The Original Script Autoinstaller

Many years ago, before cPanel added its Script Library feature, Netenberg (at the time called cpanelthemes.com) came up with a way to make it easier for end users to install and remove web scripts. This was soon imitated by cPanel and other third-party developers, but Fantastico has evolved to maintain its lead over competitors. It remains the leading third-party add-on.

Installing scripts by yourself can be a bit daunting if you don't know what you are doing. Fantastico takes all the hard work out of installing many popular scripts. Just select an item you want to install, answer a few simple questions, and then follow the instructions you are given to access your new script(s). Fantastico can both install and remove any script it supports. Fantastico also improves on cPanel's Script Library by offering features like the ability to install scripts directly in `public_html`, direct subdomain installation, tracking of all installed scripts from a single screen, automated backup of scripts before upgrading them, notification of out-of-date scripts, and so on. To learn more about Fantastico visit `http://netenberg.com/fantastico.php`.

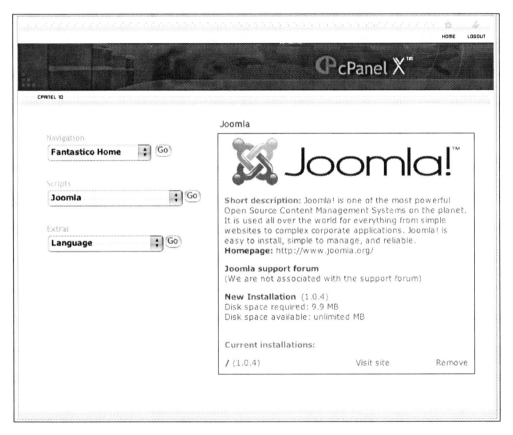

Please note that while Fantastico does offer the ability to upgrade a current Fantastico-installed version of a script to a newer version (when a new version of the script is added to Fantastico) it will remove any custom modifications you may have made to the script (although all settings will be preserved). If you don't want to lose your special modifications, visit the website of the people who maintain the script you want to update (not Netenberg's website) and look for an upgrade from your current version to whatever the latest version is.

When you click on the Fantastico icon, if you have any Fantastico-installed scripts that Fantastico has a newer version of, you will be prompted to upgrade your older versions. Fantastico upgrades work by completely backing up your current version of the installed script (including the MySQL database if needed) and then installing a clean copy of the new script and then importing all your old settings and MySQL database data. If the import goes well, then the old script is deleted and the backup retained, just in case. You can use this compressed backup to manually downgrade later if needed or to copy over modifications from your old install to your new install. This backup will be kept for a while and then Fantastico will prompt you to delete the backup if you no longer want/need it. This makes the upgrade process very safe.

Fantastico's interface is available in a number of languages (see the option in the Extras area). Choosing a language here only affects the text in Fantastico's interface (and e-mails). It does not affect what language the script you've chosen is installed in. Each script may or may not have languages other than English available, but this depends on the developer of the script and not Fantastico.

After installation, Fantastico offers to send an e-mail with the installation details to an e-mail address you specify. This e-mail contains a handy reminder of what was installed and where it was installed so you can refer to it later.

Fantastico is updated often with new versions of scripts, additional features, or new scripts, so it is a good idea to click Fantastico often to see if there is anything new available.

Web hosts and resellers have the ability to upgrade a customer's installed scripts via Fantastico by logging into the cPanel account with their reseller or root password and selecting a script to upgrade in Fantastico. Web hosts and resellers cannot install new scripts, only upgrade or remove existing scripts unless they know their customer's cPanel password.

Autoinstaller: More Scripts for cPanel's Script Library

Autoinstaller by cpSkins.com is an alternative to Fantastico. It offers many of the same scripts as Fantastico as well as a few extra. It relies on the standard cPanel Scripts Library installer interface and therefore is compatible with any theme that supports the Scripts Library feature. However, it also shares the Scripts Library limitations (you cannot install the scripts in web root and they cannot be installed in subdomains). Autoinstaller scripts are updated periodically, so you should check the installation page in Scripts Library for updates. Autoinstaller does not back up scripts that it updates, so you should make a backup before trying to apply any update.

OpenInstaller: Additional Script Library Scripts, for Free

OpenInstaller (http://openinstaller.com/) is yet another project that offers more scripts for the cPanel Scripts Library. The OpenInstaller script installer modules are free, but are rarely updated.

MailScanner cPanel Front End: Kill E-mail Nuisances before they Reach your In-Box

MailScanner (http://sng.ecs.soton.ac.uk/mailscanner/) is a technology that automatically scans all mail for not only viruses (if your web host has this installed), but also scans for spam using SpamAssassin (which can also include some custom rulesets and other anti-spam plug-ins), phishing attacks, web bugs, and other e-mail exploits.

The MailScanner front end for cPanel is maintained by http://configserver.com/. This interface replaces cPanel's standard SpamAssassin and SpamBox features as well as cPanel Pro's ClamAV virus scanner and provides additional features you just don't get with cPanel's standard features.

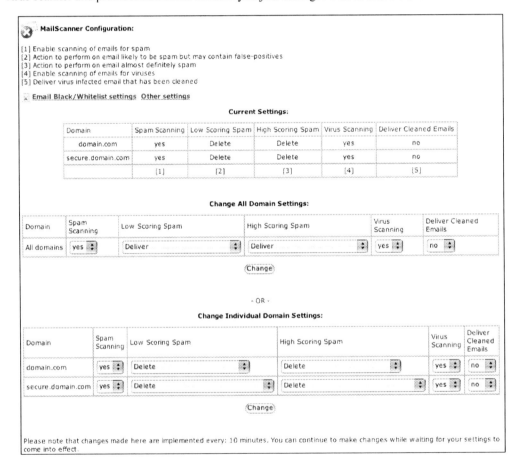

Clicking on the MailScanner icon brings you to the screen you see opposite. This screen may look a little intimidating at first, but once you take the time to explore, you'll find that it is quite easy to use.

Exploring MailScanner Front End's Many Features

At the top of the screen, you will see a numerical legend that is used in the tables here. Just below that are the links to the e-mail black/white list and other settings. Just below those links are the current MailScanner settings for your domain(s) and subdomains.

If you do nothing, e-mail will be scanned for viruses by default and any messages with viruses will be immediately deleted without being delivered. Checks for spam will also be run, but all spam will be delivered normally to your e-mail accounts (the subject line will be modified to note if the message is probably spam so you can filter it). If you do not like these defaults, you can change them for all domains and subdomains at once or have different settings for each domain or subdomain.

The next table is titled Change All Domain Settings and is used if you need to make changes to all domains and subdomains that are part of this cPanel account. The first column notes that this will affect all domains and subdomains.

Spam Scanning: The second column allows you to set whether incoming e-mail is scanned for spam or not (outgoing mail is always scanned for spam and viruses regardless of the settings here).

Low Scoring Spam: This column affects what happens if SpamAssassin decides a message is low-scoring spam and spam scanning is on. Low-scoring spam is probably spam, but might also be legitimate e-mail. A message is low-scoring spam if it scores above the minimum low-scoring spam threshold (which can be set in the Other Settings screen discussed later) but that is less than the minimum high-scoring spam threshold (which can also be set in the Other Setting screen). The default low-scoring spam threshold number is five and the default high-scoring spam threshold is twenty. This means that if SpamAssassin score is more than 5 and less than twenty, the message will be considered to be low-scoring spam by default. You can choose to deliver the spam, delete it, or forward it to a particular e-mail address.

- Deliver sends the scored e-mail with a modified subject and headers to your inbox. You can then use standard cPanel mail filters on the mail or have your e-mail client take care of sorting the spam. Low-scoring spam will have {Spam?} added to the beginning of the subject line so it is easier to filter out.

- Delete immediately deletes the mail once it has been determined to be spam. The mail is not bounced back to the sender; it is simply deleted without any other notice.

- Forward to spam@(sub.)domain.com sends the mail to that address rather than delivering it to the intended address. This allows you to duplicate the SpamBox feature that cPanel normally has, but with more control. If you choose this, you should either create a forwarding address for spam@domain.com or create a real e-mail POP3/IMAP account so the spam has some place to go. Since you can create a forwarder for this address, you can forward spam to as many other locations as you want, by creating a forwarder that sends to multiple addresses. For example, if you have a spamcop.net account, you can forward the mail to SpamCop for processing. For this option, the e-mail address is always set to spam@domain.com or spam@sub.domain.com; you cannot change the actual address listed here.

- Forward to other@domain.com may also be listed as an option if you've specified another e-mail address to forward mail to in the Other Settings area. This e-mail address can be any address at any domain; it doesn't have to be some domain hosted by you.

High-Scoring Spam: High-scoring spam is almost certainly real spam. By default, that is any e-mail message with a SpamAssassin score of 20 or higher (which you can change in the Other Settings area). You have exactly the same options as for low-scoring spam: deliver, delete or forward the mail. Delivered high-scoring spam will have {Definitely Spam?} added at the beginning of the subject line so you can filter it out using cPanel mail filters or your e-mail client's filters. We recommend that you delete high scoring spam.

Virus Scanning: Turns virus scanning on or off. Virus scans are done by ClamAV (or whichever virus scanner your web host has installed).

Deliver Cleaned E-mails: Most virus scanners have the ability to attempt to clean attachments that contain viruses. It is quite rare these days that an infected attachment can be successfully cleaned. For this reason, you should choose not to deliver cleaned e-mails.

If you make changes to any settings, be sure to click the Change button under the table you made changes in.

> Changes to MailScanner settings are not applied immediately. There can be a ten-minute wait before your new settings become active.

Below the Change All Domains Settings table is the Change Individual Domain Settings table, which allows you to make the same changes as above to each domain or subdomain separately.

Near the top of the screen, just under the numerical legend, are two links, each leading to a separate page.

MailScanner Configuration:

Whitelisted addresses will always be delivered blacklisted addresses will always be marked as High Scoring Spam

Spam Whitelist:
admin@domain.com

Spam Blacklist:

Maximum Entries: 1/30   Maximum Entries: 0/30
Allowed Format: *@domain.com or name@domain.com, only one entry per line

(Change)

[Back to MailScanner Configuration]
[Back to cPanel]

E-mail Black/Whitelist Settings: On this screen, you can set up e-mail addresses or even entire domains that you either do or do not want mail from. Any addresses in the spam whitelist won't be scanned by SpamAssassin but will be scanned for viruses and if the message does not contain a virus, it will be immediately delivered to the appropriate mail account. This is great if you want to make sure mail from a particular domain or e-mail address is never accidentally labeled as spam. On the other hand, any addresses or domains in the spam blacklist will automatically be labeled by MailScanner as high-scoring spam, and the appropriate action based on your preferences will be taken.

✗ MailScanner Configuration:

⊠ You should be very careful about changing the spam score detection settings, the defaults are recommended. The low spam score must be lower than the high spam score.

Low scoring spam setting	5 default ▲▼
High scoring spam setting	20 default ▲▼
Additional email address to list for forwarding spam	spam@otherdomain.com

(Change)

[Back to MailScanner Configuration]

[Back to cPanel]

Other Settings: This screen allows you to edit a few settings you probably won't need to change very often, if at all. You can set the minimum SpamAssassin score needed for a piece of mail to be categorized as low- or high-scoring spam and you can also specify a different e-mail address that you want as an option to forward low- or high-scoring spam to. Keep in mind that the address specified here will appear as an option for both high- and low-scoring spam for all domains and subdomains along with the standard spam@(sub.)domain.com. Be sure to click Change if you make any changes. The new high- and low-scoring spam settings will take up to 10 minutes to become active, but the e-mail address you specify here will become an option immediately.

How does MailScanner Handle Mail?

For all incoming mail (including mail for forwarding addresses):

- The mail is initially scanned by the mail server to figure out whom it is for.

- MailScanner looks up the domain or subdomain settings and scans the mail message for viruses first (if enabled by the user or web host). If no settings exist, the defaults are used (spam and virus scanning on with viruses being deleted and spam being tagged and delivered). Compressed attachments (`.zip`, `.rar`, `.sit`, and so on) are scanned for viruses as well.

- If the mail message contains a virus, immediate action is taken based on the domain MailScanner Configuration or your web host's settings.

- If the virus is set to be cleaned and delivered, the message may be tagged as having a virus {virus?} and the attachment is cleaned if possible. You should be very careful with these attachments since very few viruses can be successfully cleaned out of attachments.

- The message is scanned by MailScanner and then SpamAssassin to determine if it is spam (if that feature is turned on for the receiving domain).

- Depending on the SpamAssassin score, the message is processed and tagged according to the domain's settings.

- MailScanner looks for evidence of phishing attacks, web bugs, external message bodies, banned attachment types, and other dangerous content based on your web host's settings.

- MailScanner can look for links that claim to point to one destination while actually taking the user to another site. These sorts of links might be part of a phishing attack. MailScanner has a built-in whitelist for known *good* sites. If the link is for a site not on the whitelist, MailScanner rewrites all such e-mail links (if the message is in HTML format) so it is clear exactly where you are going if you click a particular link or image in the e-mail. Mail is never deleted simply because it contains what looks like phishing links; it is always delivered (unless the message is classified as spam or a virus, and then the action taken depends on those settings).

- Web bugs are removed and replaced with a small MailScanner graphic to note that a web bug has been removed. Removal is fairly accurate, but there is always a chance one may be missed.

- Messages with entirely external message bodies (a message that tries to connect to the Internet to pull up the entire message body from a remote location) are rejected; the message is bounced back to the sender with a note on why the message was rejected.

- If the message contains object codebase or form tags, the tags may be removed and the message is delivered per the domain settings.

- Banned attachment types cause the message to be bounced back to the sender with a note about why the message was rejected. If a user needs to send a banned attachment type, they should compress the file or files and the message will go through.

For outgoing mail the process is similar, except:

- All outgoing mail is typically scanned for viruses and spam regardless of incoming mail domain settings. Viruses are immediately deleted by default. Spam may be scored and sent on. If real spam is sent from a domain on your server, it will be easy to track back to the source this way.

- Outgoing mail is not subject to your domain spam white- or blacklists.

Although this is typically how MailScanner handles mail, MailScanner is constantly updated with new and improved features and your web host will have complete control over the process, so it may be different than described here. Contact your web host if you have questions.

Other Third-Party Add-ons

A number of companies offer other add-ons for (or products that work with) cPanel, a few of which are listed here:

Site Studio (`http://psoft.net/SS/site_studio_info.html`): A Java-based site builder program that integrates with the cPanel user database if you want it to.

SiteBuilderCX (`http://sitebuildercx.com/`): A site-building program made especially for cPanel. It integrates directly with cPanel and can be accessed from there.

Click Be!: A site-building program from the makers of Fantastico (`http://netenberg.com/`), it can be integrated with cPanel but does not require it.

RVsitebuilder: This is a site builder from the makers of RVSKIN (`http://rvsitebuilder.com/`). It can be integrated with cPanel though it does not require either cPanel or RVSKIN.

cpShout (`http://cpshout.com/`): Allows users to stream audio via shoutcast.

ShoutCast Panel (`http://scpanel.net/`): Another product that integrates with cPanel and allows the user to stream audio via shoutcast.

Summary

In this chapter, you discovered the many themes that your web host can offer and learned a bit about the special features they may offer. In addition, we explored many of the most popular third-party add-ons and learned how several of them work including Fantastico and the cPanel MailScanner front end.

In the final chapter, we will explore some links to popular and important tools for webmasters.

13

Useful Tools and Links and the Final Curtain Call

Congratulations! You've managed to hang in there and you've reached the final chapter of this book. cPanel is a complex tool, but you've taken the first few steps towards mastery by reading this book. Hopefully, you have a much better sense of what cPanel is capable of doing and how you can use it to create and manage your own website.

Now your task is about to begin (if it hasn't already). It's up to you to create the very best, most vibrant and alive web presence you can. Before you put down the book there are a few last items you may want to peruse. In particular, I will list a few common tools that many expert web masters rely on, to get you started. Feel free to explore and find some of your own. Let me know if you find any other great tools out there and perhaps I'll add them to future editions of this book.

You will find several great links for tools you can use for:

- FTP clients
- Additional cPanel information
- Basic webmaster and scripting assistance
- Domain, DNS, and site monitoring tools
- Password storing programs

So let's get to them!

FTP Clients

One of the most important things you can do for yourself is ditch your web browser when trying to upload or download files to your account. Take the time to find an S/FTP client that you feel comfortable with. The following list is by no means complete, but it lists several popular FTP clients for a number of computing platforms.

Operating System(s) Supported	FTP Client Name	URL	Notes
Windows 95 – XP	FileZilla	`http://filezilla.sourceforge.net/`	Free, popular.
Windows 3.1 – XP	WS_FTP Pro	`http://ipswitch.com/Products/file-transfer.html`	34.95 – 84.95 USD depending on version and service agreement.
Windows 95 – XP / Mac OS 8.5 – X 10.4	CuteFTP	`http://globalscape.com/products/ftp_clients.asp`	39.99 – 99.99 USD depending on configuration. Also available in a Macintosh version.
Mac OS X 10.1 – 10.4	Rbrowser	`http://rbrowser.com/`	Available in a free version or a 35 USD paid edition with many more features.
Mac OS 9.x – X 10.4	Transmit	`http://panic.com/transmit/`	29.95 USD.
Mac OS 7 – X10.4	Fetch	`http://fetchsoftworks.com/`	25 USD – One of the very first Mac OS FTP clients.
Linux/Windows	Igloo Pro	`http://iglooftp.com/linux/index.html`	29.95 USD – Yes, Linux Shareware! Also comes in a Windows version.

Additional cPanel Information

If you need additional assistance with cPanel, here are a few places you can turn to for help.

Resource Name	URL	Notes
Official cPanel Documentation	`http://cpanel.net/docs/cpanel/`	This is the same documentation as is available via a link in cPanel. Nearly all features are covered, but not in much depth.
Official cPanel Forum	`http://forums.cpanel.net/`	A great place for assistance with cPanel. There are always people willing to help. This forum is not designed for official support from cPanel Inc., but they do often respond to threads.
Your web hosting company	Varies	Your web host is there to help you if you have questions.

Basic Webmaster and Scripting Assistance

If you need help putting together your website or working with scripts, here are a few places that can teach you more:

Resource Name	URL	Notes
HTML Basix	`http://htmlbasix.com/`	This site offers numerous tutorials on HTML and building websites. It also includes several tools to automatically create custom code for your site.
W3 Schools	`http://w3schools.com/`	If you want to learn anything about HTML or other web technologies (PHP, CSS, etc.), this is the place to do that free.
W3C Validator	`http://validator.w3.org/`	Use this tool to make sure your site's (X)HTML, XML or CSS is coded properly. This helps you avoid browser rendering issues.
Lisa Explains HTML	`http://lissaexplains.com/`	This site focuses on teaching HTML to kids.
Free Webmaster Help	`http://freewebmasterhelp.com/`	Free tutorials, tools, and templates for web masters.
Hot Scripts	`http://hotscripts.com/`	An excellent directory of scripts available in many different programming languages. Many of them are free.
CGI Directory	`http://cgidir.com/`	Similar to Hot Scripts, but it focuses on CGI scripts.
Free Web Templates	`http://freewebtemplates.com/`	Use templates as the base for your website so you can focus on content. This site has plenty of free templates anyone can use.
Open Source Web Design	`http://oswd.org/`	Thousands of free templates you can use on your own site.
Templates Resource	`http://templatesresource.com/`	The templates here aren't free, but if you are looking for something unique, 39.95 USD gets you access to thousands of templates and logos.
Template Monster	`http://templatemonster.com/`	Reasonably priced templates, plus you can purchase exclusive rights to many templates so no one else can use the same one as you.

Domain, DNS, and Site Monitoring Tools

Even the most reliable hosts sometimes have issues beyond their control. If your website is important to you then you will find these services immensely handy.

Resource Name	URL	Notes
Site Uptime	`http://siteuptime.com/`	Sign up on this site and they will monitor your website free and notify you if your site is inaccessible for any reason. If you need more frequent monitoring, you can pay for an advanced, or premium account.
Alertra	`http://alertra.com/`	Free *on demand* check of your website to make sure it is up. For a fee, Alertra can also watch your site to make sure it stays online.

Resource Name	URL	Notes
No-IP	http://no-ip.com/	Free dynamic DNS resolution (handy if you're trying to host a website or files from your home computer). They also offer a wide variety of services for a fee, including backup name servers, mail service, mail redirection, and spam filtering.
Gradwell Ltd.	http://gradwell.com/	Offers backup name service, mail service, and even hosting.
DNS Stuff	http://dnsstuff.com/	A wide variety of DNS tools. This can be very handy if you are having problems accessing your site and think the problem might be DNS-related.
DNS Report	http://dnsreport.com/	Receive a full report on the entries in your site's DNS zone. If there are any problems, this should flush them out and also tell you what to do about it.
Whois.sc	http://whois.sc/	Performs a "whois" on the domain name or IP address you enter. This can tell you who owns a site, who to contact about it, where it is hosted, and other interesting information.
Sam Spade	http://samspade.org/	Numerous DNS and Internet-related tools.

Password Storing Programs

In order to keep the passwords you use both random and strong you need some safe location to store this information unless you have a picture-perfect memory. Just be careful to always keep a secure, recent backup of your passwords and make sure the password you use to access these tools is long, random and yet something you will not forget.

Resource Name	URL	Notes
Web Confidential	http://web-confidential.com/	Secure password storage program for Windows, Mac OS, and Palm OS. Password files can be shared between all platforms. $20 Mac/Windows, $15 Palm, or $45 for all three.
Pass Vault	http://digisafe.com/products/products_PassVault.htm	Designed specially for use and storage on removable media (like USB flash drives). Works with Windows only. $29.99.
PasswordSafe	http://schneier.com/passsafe.html	Free open source Windows password manager. It also has related projects for Mac OS X, Linux, Palm OS, and Pocket PC that can read and write the same password database file format, so you can use one database on all platforms. The user interface could use some work, but the price is right.
Figaro's Password Manager	http://fpm.sourceforge.net/	A free Linux/Unix (with GNOME) password manager.

Curtain Call

I would like to thank you for buying and/or reading this book and hope you will take the time to let me know any thoughts you might have on concerning it. If you have any feedback, please send it to the address given in the introduction.

Remember! Books are great tools, but if you need immediate help with your hosting account or cPanel, always discuss the matter with your web host. Chances are they can help you quickly resolve any issue you might be having before it becomes a serious problem.

A
Glossary

Add-on Domain: Another domain (domain2.com) added to a cPanel account that acts as if it is separate from the main domain that cPanel manages (domain.com).

Anonymous FTP: This allows people without FTP accounts to access a special directory to upload or download files.

Apache Handlers: Handlers tell the web server itself how to handle certain types of files (.html, .cgi, .pl, and so on).

Apache: Common, free web page serving software.

Backup: The process of copying important data in case the original data becomes damaged or goes missing for some reason. Used as a noun it refers to the data that has been backed up.

Bandwidth: A measure of how much data is transferred to or from your website, e-mail, or FTP hosting account. Typically, this is measured in computer gigabytes (1 GB = 1,024 MB).

Bounced E-mail: E-mail messages that get returned to the sender because there was some sort of problem and the e-mail could not be delivered.

CGI (Common Gateway Interface): The interface that allows external applications to access web servers. Depending on the setup of the web server, some programming languages can only be accessed via CGI (for example, Perl or Python).

ClamAV: A free open-source virus scanner.

cPanel: A popular web-based hosting control software package. The company that develops this software also goes by the same name. It is called cPanel Inc.

Cron Jobs: Commands or web scripts that the web server executes at a particular time.

Database (MySQL or PostgreSQL): Databases are used to store information for quick retrieval. Many web scripts require the use of at least one database.

Dedicated Server: An entire web server (physical machine) with no accounts on it that you can use to sell shared or reseller hosting or use for some other purpose if you choose.

Disk Space: This is a measure of how much stuff you can store on a server or in your hosting account. Disk space is usually measured in computer megabytes (1 MB = 1024 Kb).

DNS (Domain Name Service): The system that allows domain names to be translated into their corresponding IP addresses (111.111.111.111).

Domain Name: The name of a website or location on the Internet. A domain name resolves to an IP address via DNS.

DOS (Denial of Service) Attack: This sort of attack uses many computers to flood your web server with fake requests for information with the hope of taking the server or your site off the Internet.

E-mail Address: This is what people type in to send an e-mail to you. For example, user@domain.com. E-mail addresses always include the @ (at sign).

E-mail Alias/Forwarder: An e-mail address that sends e-mail automatically to another e-mail address or addresses without storing the e-mail.

E-mail Body: The main section of the e-mail with whatever text you have written.

E-mail Filter: A filter takes action by redirecting, deleting, or storing incoming e-mail based on criteria you set.

E-mail Headers: Several lines of information that appear prior to the body of an e-mail message. The headers contain a lot of information about where the mail has come from and which mail server received it. Most e-mail programs don't show full headers by default since there can be so many of them. If you are having problems with spam or bounced e-mail messages, the full headers of the message contain information that can help track down the problem.

E-mail: Electronic messages.

FrontPage Extensions: Special code that runs on a web server to enable additional features in Microsoft's FrontPage HTML editor program. Do not enable the FrontPage extensions unless you plan to use Microsoft FrontPage exclusively to edit your website. The extensions interfere with other features that cPanel and Apache offer.

FTP (File Transfer Protocol): A protocol for transferring and working with files and directories on a remote server.

FTP Client: A program used to work with files on a remote server via FTP or SFTP.

FXP (File eXchange Protcol): FXP is FTP directly between two separate FTP accounts you are logged into in via your FTP client.

Hacker: Individuals who attempt to disrupt websites and computer systems illegally.

Hit: A request for a web page or other content on your website.

Hotlink Protection: Stops other people on other websites linking directly to your files unless they have approval from you to do so.

HTML: The programming language most web pages are written in.

IMAP: This is a protocol for fetching e-mail from a remote web server. IMAP is designed to manage all mail on the remote mail server. IMAP is a good protocol to use if you travel a lot and want to be able to access all of your mail from anywhere. However, if your mail server is having problems you likely won't be able to access any mail (even old mail) until the server comes back online.

Index Page: On most websites, the index page (`index.html`, `index.htm`) is the first page accessed when someone visits that domain or subdomain.

IP Address: The number assigned to an item accessible on the Internet (or on a private network). IP addresses currently are a series of four three-digit numbers separated by periods (111.111.111.111).

Kernel: The core of the Linux operating system.

Leech Protection: Stop users with valid user logins from giving out their access to anyone else. Leech Protection disables a user's access if it is used too many times to access your site or protected material. It works with the Apache password-protected directory feature.

Mailbox: The location where mail is stored for an e-mail address.

MIME Types: MIME stands for Multipurpose Internet Mail Extensions. MIME types let a user's web browser know what a given file is so that it knows how to handle that file (display it, download it, pass it to a browser plug-in, and so on).

MX (Mail Exchange) Record: An MX record tells the server where e-mail for a particular domain should be sent.

Parked Domain: A domain that mirrors the content of the main domain managed in cPanel.

Password Authentication: This is one method you can use to prove that the e-mail account is yours. You enter your account username and password.

Password Protected Directories: Apache can require that users log in before accessing a particular directory of your website. People without valid log-in credentials will be denied access.

Perl: A programming language used by some web scripts.

PGP (Pretty Good Privacy): A highly secure encryption system with public and private *keys*.

PHP: A programming language that a lot of web-based scripts use.

phpMyAdmin: Web-based program that allows you to manipulate MySQL databases.

phpPgAdmin: Web-based program that allows you to manipulate PostgreSQL databases.

Ping: The amount of time (typically listed in milliseconds) that it takes for a server to respond to a request. Longer times mean the connection will be slower. Ping times can be affected by a wide range of issues, like the physical distance between you and the server itself, routing issues somewhere between the server and your current location, problems on the server or problems locally (perhaps with your ISP).

POP3: This is a protocol for fetching e-mail from a mail server. This method was designed to retrieve mail from a remote mail server and store the e-mail locally. Mail fetched via POP3 typically gets removed from a server once your e-mail client has fetched the mail (though you can change this behavior). Since mail is removed from the server, you typically can only read old mail in the e-mail program used to download the messages. If your mail server goes down, you will still be able to access old mail locally without an Internet connection.

POP-Before-SMTP Authentication: An alternative SMTP (send mail) authentication method. To use this method, you must log in to your e-mail account via POP3 and check your e-mail. If you do that successfully then you will be able to send e-mail from that account for 30 minutes via SMTP without having to enter the account username and password again. This is a somewhat less secure than password authentication and not all web hosts support it.

Proxy: A program, service, or script that allows you to access content from one location through another. The cPanel proxy script allows accessing cPanel, webmail, and WHM via the standard web port (80) so you can access them in locations that don't allow access to the standard ports.

Python: A programming language some web scripts are written in.

Raw Web Log: The log created by Apache as users access websites on the web server.

Redirect: A redirect sends anyone who accesses a web page to a new location. Redirects come in two forms, temporary and permanent. A temporary redirect is used for content that may have moved to a new location, but isn't going to be there forever (useful for search engine indexing). A permanent redirect tells search engines that the new location is permanent and they should update their records and stop linking to the old URI for that resource.

Reseller Hosting: Reseller hosting is similar to shared hosting, except that you are allowed to resell shared hosting accounts to others.

Session: The entire contiguous period of time that a user visits your website before leaving it to go elsewhere.

SFTP: A secure (encrypted) version of the FTP protocol.

Shared Hosting: Many websites hosted on a single web server.

SMTP (Simple Mail Transfer Protocol): SMTP is the protocol used when you need to send someone e-mail from your account.

SSH (Secure Shell): A secure protocol for interacting remotely with a computer via a text-based interface. SSH is a secure version of Telnet.

SSL (Secure Socket Layer): SSL is also referred to as TLS or Transport Layer Security. It is the main protocol used on the Web to ensure that traffic to and from a website is encrypted so third parties cannot intercept data (like your credit card information).

SSL Certificate: A special file that enables SSL communication between a website and the user's web browser.

Subdomains: Subdomains are addresses like `subdomain.domain.com`. A subdomain can either act as if it were an entirely different site, not part of your primary domain (using the Add-on Domain feature discussed in Chapter 10) or it can serve as a *shortcut* to redirect you to another place either in your site or to anywhere on the Internet.

Telnet: An insecure (unencrypted) protocol for interacting remotely with a computer via a text-based interface. Telnet has largely been subsumed by SSH, a secure version of the Telnet protocol.

Theme: A unique visual look to a program or web page. A cPanel theme also can offer additional features and functionality.

TLS (Transport Layer Security): See the definition for SSL.

Traceroute: The traceroute command lists the route your data would take between your computer and the domain that you type in. Each stop on the trip will list the response time (ping) from each server in milliseconds. Lower numbers are better; high numbers mean your connection may be adversely affected.

VPS/VDS Hosting: VPS (Virtual Private Server) or VDS (Virtual Dedicated Server) hosting are different names for the same type of hosting accounts. Such accounts use special software to take a single physical web server and divide it into 2 or more separate virtual web servers. Each virtual server acts as if it is a completely separate machine.

Web Mail (Client): A program that allows you to access your e-mail from a web browser.

Web Scripts: Programs that run via a web browser over the Internet.

Web Server: A machine that serves web pages and other content on the Internet. Also the software (like Apache) that actually does the serving.

Web Stat(istics) Program: A program like Analog, Webalizer, or AWSTATS that interprets the raw data in the Apache raw web logs and condenses that information into useful charts and graphs.

Web Statistics: Basic information about where your visitors came from, how they found your site and what sort of computer and browser they used during the visit. This information comes from the Apache raw web log.

Webmaster: The person (or people) responsible for the content and running of a website.

WHM (Web Hosting Manager): This is a companion program that comes with cPanel that allows server administrators to manage the server and accounts and allows resellers to manage accounts.

Index

Printed in the United Kingdom
by Lightning Source UK Ltd.
134176UK00001B/286/A